PRAISE FOR *THE PARENTS' GUI*

M000291032

The authors of The Parents' Guide to Raising CEO Kids masterfully weave parenting, life, business, and financial principles and skills into a practical, actionable handbook. By interviewing successful CEO kids and their parents, this deeply-researched read is essential for any parent who wants to fully prepare their children to thrive in our ever-changing, global economy. But this book isn't just for parents. I predict a lot of entrepreneurial kids will read and then train their parents on the concepts in this book, and these kids will be inspired by the advice and success stories so well presented.

Ken Kaufman, funder & CEO of <u>CFOwise</u>® and the author of
Impact Your Business

The Parents' Guide to Raising CEO Kids gives parents guidance and kids the tools to succeed. As parents we need to empower our kids by giving them support and encouragement. How do you do that if you have never run a business yourself? Even if you do, modeling the behavior is not enough to give them the confidence they need. Supporting our children's vision, mapping a plan of action, understanding their attitude and commitment and instilling the confidence they need to have their desired outcome is what this book is all about. The stories of the CEO kids interviewed within will make you shake your head in amazement and applaud their ingenuity. Give your kids the first steps to climb that ladder of their own success and empower yourselves as parents to confidently support their dreams.

Dori DeCarlo, founder of S1 Safety First, LLC and host of *Word of Mom* radio show

The
Parents' Guide
to

Raising
CEO
Kids

Dr. Jerry Cook
Sarah L. Cook
Founder, Raising CEO Kids

Published and distributed in the United States by:
C Collaborative, LLC,
P.O. Box 7172-334 Stateline, NV 89449-7172
775-629-2836
www.ccollaborativellc.com

Raising CEO Kids is a registered trademark of C Collaborative, LLC.

Editor: Karen Grove   www.karengrove.com

Cover Design: Chaz DeSimone   www.chazdesimone.com

Creative Concept and Creative Consultant: Nancy O'Neill
                                                                www.onedotenterprises.com

Interior Design: Bobbie Smith   www.missbobbie.com

Photography of the Cook Family: Merilee Blake

For general information on Raising CEO Kids, its products, services, and youth entrepreneur interviews, please visit www.RaisingCEOKids.com

ISBN 13: 978-0-98-6880-3-7

ISBN 10: 0-9836880-3-6

1. Parenting   2. Entrepreneurship   3. Business Life

1st printing, August 2011

Printed in the United States of America

DEDICATION

The Parents' Guide to Raising CEO Kids is dedicated to Jacob, Clarissa, and Jonathan Cook, our three children and young entrepreneurs. Each of you bless our lives, family, and the world at large with the gifts you so freely share. We love you.

ACKNOWLEDGEMENTS

This book would never have been possible without the support and input of hundreds of people.

Nearly 200 young entrepreneurs and their parents - Allowing us to interview you made the book a reality. Thank you for your excellence in all you do, and for allowing us to look inside your life, business, and family dynamics to learn from you.

The Raising CEO Kids community - Thank you for cheering us on via the Facebook "Like" page, email, Skype, letters and the phone. You kept us going.

Nancy O'Neill, The Common Sense Coach - Your unwavering commitment to us and to this project is priceless. Thank you for your friendship and the countless phone calls and emails of encouragement.

Chaz DeSimone - For accepting nothing less than perfection for our logo and cover. Thank you for bringing it all together so well.

Sweetie Berry - Thank you for your vision of what is possible and for your insight on the strategy for how to get there.

Karen Grove - Your editing brilliance shines in this book. Thank you for your dedication to the completion of *The Parents' Guide to Raising CEO Kids*.

Bobbie Smith – Your dedication to excellence in your personal life and professional work leaves us awed and inspired. Thank you for being you.

Carol and David Bastow - For keenly remembering every special occasion and for being there during each bump in the road. We love you for always.

Katie Simmons - For your Godly heart and your willingness to go the extra mile behind-the-scenes. We are so grateful for you.

Shaena Babcock – For being a fabulous intern during the wrapping-up stages of our book. You have a phenomenal attitude, and we wish you every success.

The Social Media World - To the thousands of people around the world who have tweeted, messaged, "Liked," or in any way shown your support, we thank you!

Contents

PREFACE

Youth have more potential than society gives them credit for. There are so many things that fuel negativity and pessimism among the young, and that teach them they are worth little and can accomplish less. Many of the institutions designed to transform our youth into successful, happy, and well-adjusted adults have failed them. These same institutions are failing us all because we will depend on the youth in the not-so-distant future. This book was created to inspire, educate, and empower young people and the adults who raise and mentor them with the understanding and knowledge that the potential and capabilities of youth are limitless.

Personal circumstances led to the formation of Raising CEO Kids. The seeds were planted when our oldest son began studying the value of Pokémon cards and trading them to his advantage with friends. This led to his desire to sell them, and eventually to sell other items online for a large profit. At first, we said "no", believing that the Internet was no place for children. After months of listening to our persistent son, we reached an epiphany. Perhaps, as parents of three children, we were not believing enough in him and his siblings. We began to put in place practices to better foster their dreams and goals. It wasn't as if we had wanted our children to fail; it was more like our own fears of failing had created a fear of seeing them fail. As time went on, their inspiration, persistence, and courage motivated us to take more and more action to support and empower them, and in that process a movement was fueled.

> **Imagine what the world would be like if each person had the opportunity to develop their gifts and turn their gifts and passion into profit.**

With enthusiasm to support and empower our own children, we researched and found hundreds of other youth who demonstrated the same remarkable characteristics and entrepreneurial spirit we were seeing in our own household. Sarah interviewed more than 150 of these young entrepreneurs, as well as a majority of their parents, and has been sharing the interviews on http://raisingceokids.com/category/ceo-kids/. Hundreds of hours of transcription and examination led us to some fabulous insights. The underlying characteristics found in all of the youth interviewed were things that could be learned, that parents could teach, and that society would benefit from. Empowering youth with a purpose for life, joy-filled work, a positive attitude, and a goal-oriented framework became our vision, and one we seek to share with others. This book focuses on how to raise young entrepreneurs, but it is also a great resource for youth who want to deepen and increase their life purpose, achieve their dreams, and make a difference in the world.

In this book, you will be given the most comprehensive framework for helping the youth entrepreneur to not only build a profitable business, but also the person behind that business. In our research, we identified many of the challenges that need to be overcome as well as the resources you will need to overcome them more easily and quickly—so that you can spend time focusing on the things you value most.

> **We asked Mr. Evers, father of Austin Evers, youth entrepreneur and founder of Appuous Inc., "If you could have had resources available to help you in raising entrepreneur kids, what would you have wanted?" He replied, "We needed a solid resource where we could have learned about doing all of this—that would have greatly helped. And we believe what you are doing with Raising CEO Kids is just that."**

Foreword for *The Parents' Guide to Raising CEO Kids*
Robert Brooks, Ph.D.

I was trained as a clinical psychologist in the late 1960s and early 1970s. It was a period when mental health professionals routinely focused on "fixing" the problems of their patients. Only lip service was given to identifying and reinforcing the strengths that resided in each individual. An adherence to this so-called "deficit model" impacted on the questions that clinicians asked and the strategies they applied in their practices.

Those of us who worked with children and adolescents typically exhausted most sessions asking parents as well as their children about the problems the latter were experiencing. Little, if any, time was spent inquiring about the youngster's interests, passions, or strengths. Even less time was afforded asking parents about what they viewed as their own strengths. While it is necessary to address problems and symptoms, to do so without identifying and fortifying strengths produces a very narrow, shortsighted approach. It lessens the impact clinicians can have to help both children and adults lead a more meaningful, satisfying life.

In the 1970s, especially based on my clinical experiences working with youth in the inner city of Boston and then at McLean Hospital, a private psychiatric hospital, my focus began to change. I began to raise certain questions, including, "Why is it that some children can grow up under racism or poverty or grow up in abusive or chaotic homes or grow up with life-threatening illnesses and yet cope successfully with these difficulties to lead lives filled with positive relationships, satisfying jobs, and a sense of optimism and hope?" Little did I realize that the seeds of my interest in the concept of *resilience* were being planted, seeds that were to flourish not only as important features of my career but also in the field of mental health as evidenced by the emergence of "positive psychology."

Studies in the area of resilience initially focused on children who had overcome great adversity. Clinicians and researchers were interested in identifying the factors that led some children to cope more effectively with hardship, while other children were burdened by stress and emotional difficulties.

Variables such as the inborn temperament of children, their problem-solving skills, the style and encouragement of parents, and support outside of the immediate family were noted as key factors in determining successful adaptation.

In my collaboration with Dr. Sam Goldstein, which has included co-authoring the books *Raising Resilient Children* and *Raising a Self-Disciplined Child*, we examined factors that contributed to resilience. We identified key characteristics of what we labeled a *resilient mindset*, that is, those assumptions, expectations, and skills associated with children who had dealt successfully with adversity. Our work prompted us to wonder: "If we are aware of the characteristics of a resilient mindset, can parents reinforce these characteristics in their children from a very early age, whether or not the child has faced unusual adversity or not?" Stated somewhat differently, "Can we use what we have learned from children experiencing hardship and turmoil and apply the principles to all children regardless of the amount of stress or pressure they have encountered?"

We answered these questions in the affirmative, believing that the nurturance of a resilient mindset was of paramount importance in helping children to become more hopeful, successful, and resilient. While we emphasized that possessing such a mindset would be invaluable if and when children face unexpected stress and trauma, it also provides an outlook and skills that will help children to experience greater achievement and satisfaction at any age.

Another key finding in the resilience literature is that a resilient mindset and lifestyle are not rooted in exceptional qualities possessed by only a few fortunate children but rather are inherent in all youngsters. Psychologist Ann Masten refers to the process of resilience as "ordinary magic." It is our position that all children possess strengths or "islands of competence," a metaphor I first introduced 30 years ago. These strengths can be nurtured each and every day by parents or other caregivers. The late psychologist Julius Segal emphasized that children require "charismatic adults" in their lives, that is, adults from whom they "gather strength," to promote resilience.

As I read Jerry and Sarah Cook's very impressive book *The Parents' Guide to Raising CEO Kids*, I was constantly reminded of the strategies that Sam Goldstein and I recommend for raising caring, self-disciplined, productive, resilient children. Jerry and Sarah's appreciation of the power of parents to have an immense positive impact on a child's life is evident on every page of this book. Their respect for the capacity of children—when encouraged and guided by the "charismatic adults" in their lives—to realize noteworthy accomplishments is in refreshing contrast to the many negative articles describing the seeming lack of responsibility, dedication, and compassion in today's youth.

In articulating the four pillars for raising CEO kids, not only do Jerry and Sarah offer realistic, practical guidelines for believing in and assisting our children to become successful in the business world, but these guidelines and the skills that are learned are applicable in all domains of our children's lives. The qualities of the successful child CEO—being responsible, compassionate, thoughtful, self-disciplined, using effective interpersonal and problem-solving skills, and handling both success and setbacks with calmness and dignity—are the same as those found in resilient individuals.

A list of many child CEOs with brief descriptions of their accomplishments enriches this book. It was reassuring to discover through the revealing observations of CEO kids and their parents that these youngsters come from diverse backgrounds and that their journeys truly represent the "ordinary magic" residing in so many children whose passions, visions, and actions are influenced and supported by caring adults in their lives.

One of the most important qualities of resilience is the ability to identify and expend time and energy on those factors over which one has influence and control.
As you read *The Parents' Guide to Raising CEO Kids* you will soon recognize that not only are you preparing your children to be CEOs of their own companies but very importantly, of their own lives. A resilient mindset is a wonderful gift we can reinforce in our children and in doing so we are creating a legacy about which we can be proud. I am certain that parents will often turn to this book as an important resource in creating this legacy and assuming the admirable role of a "charismatic adult" in their children's lives.
Robert Brooks, Ph.D.,
Faculty, Harvard Medical School

1

Introduction

> One of the greatest gifts we can give our children is the empowerment to create a life they love filled with purposeful enjoyable work and relationships they hold dear.

D o you have a CEO Kid or one in the making? If you have a child, then we guarantee you have a potential young entrepreneur. If you work with children, then you likely work with future entrepreneurs. If you are a kid, you have the opportunity to be a business owner—to turn your gifts, talents, and passions into profit, and to create success for yourself and also for the world!

Part of this book focuses on how to help youth develop business and money "sense", but an equal portion focuses on the process of helping each child develop the skills to become a happy, successful, and well-adjusted adult. Several of the passages in later chapters (especially Chapters 3–9) come directly from current and former CEO Kids. Their personal experience is empowering and valuable reading for young entrepreneurs.

To effectively instill the attributes needed for youth to succeed as young entrepreneurs, we must consider our own abilities as parents, educators, and government leaders. For example, it's well known that youth tend to (eventually) develop similar attitudes and morals of their parents, caregivers, mentors, and educators they spend the most time with. We must ask ourselves, "Are we unintentionally raising our children to go to a job they will hate?"

> **For youth reading this chapter, we recommend you share these facts and data with others to support you in your entrepreneurship goals. We know you can create success! Let's get started!**

Consider the importance of work in every part of your life. We need strong work ethic to be productive in our employment, to achieve our personal goals, and to establish solid connections within families and between friends. In reality, it is work and our work ethic that carries us—or burdens us—for much of our adult lives. There is no way to completely escape the power of work, nor from its ability to shape every part of who we are and how we feel about ourselves and our attitudes and feelings for others.

Let's look at working a standard career life and the meaning of jobs in our society. Assuming that an adult is employed full-time from the time they are twenty-five years old until they are sixty-five years old, that equates to forty years of employment life, or 83,200 hours (52 weeks per year x 40 hours per week x 40 years) of on-the-job experiences. In reality, most people start working, at least part-time, before they are twenty-five, and it is increasingly more common for senior citizens to postpone their retirement beyond age sixty-five, so the number of hours of employment is really much greater than the equation suggests. This equation also does not take into consideration the time preparing to go to work or the time spent traveling to and from the job. With so much of our lives invested in our employment, it seems natural to think that (a) we as a society love our work, and (b) we as a society are successful in preparing the next generation for working. Far too many people have found that neither assumption is true.

How would you respond to that statement? Do you love to work? Do you love the work that you do?

Jobs, in general, seem to compete with politics and the weather for the top thing that people complain about the most. Many individuals can't wait to get a different job, a better job, or reach retirement so that they do not have to have a job. Many do not think we can control the direction or timing of certain aspects of our employment. We want our ideas to make a difference in our workplaces, and yet our voices are often not heard. With the negative acronyms associated with J.O.B. (e.g. Journey of the Broke, Just Over Broke), it is no wonder that many dread the thought of getting a job, have stopped dreaming about loving their work, hate Mondays, and join the chorus of TGIF (Thank Goodness It's Friday) so that we "don't have to be at work" for two whole days.

How are we succeeding in preparing the next generation for employment? The sad fact is that as a society we are doing a poor job in many respects. There is a common expression, "Get good grades and go to college," with the assumption of getting a great (i.e., enjoyable and high-paying) job once one graduates from college. But how well does the current education system truly prepare people for employment? For some, it does well, while for many others, it fails. Consider the high and somewhat stagnant school dropout rates, the large percentage of college students who require remedial math and English courses, double-digit unemployment levels, staggering levels of student loan debt for college graduates, and the huge percentage of students moving back home after college because they can't afford to

> **We define success as having confidence, the ability to communicate, and joyfully using passion and vision to generate cash flow and provide service to others.**

3

make it on their own. We have a problem, and we need more than a formal education from schools and universities to empower today's youth to obtain personal sustainability and thrive.

According to the Bureau of Labor Statistics[1], the summer unemployment rate among youth, or those between sixteen and twenty-four years old, was 19.1 percent, which is reportedly the highest rate of youth unemployment since at least 1948. Teens are at particular affected, as over half of them are not *even looking* for employment, clearly because the outlook is so bad. An additional sobering reality is that "employment" counts anyone who is working for one hour or more per week. many youth are working, but hardly at all, profiting little.

It's time for a radical change in the process for how we help youth transition to adulthood. Despite a potential "A" for effort, it offers little consolation (and we shouldn't sugar coat it) that the reality is we as a society have an "F" when it comes to results. Such a change will require altering the beliefs, values, and experiences that youth receive. This kind of change in how we prepare our young people for adulthood is most likely to be successful when implemented within the home and family.

This is where Raising CEO Kids comes into the picture. We represent the best practices and strategies learned from youth and their parents who have or are successfully developing the skills and attributes to both compete within society and to contribute to a world that is starving for their talents, gifts, courage, and determination. We also strive to bring youth, and the adults raising them, the best resources in supporting youth in entrepreneurship. Many of these resources are listed at the back of this book.

There are more CEO Kids than most people may imagine, and the number is growing because of the benefits that being a CEO Kid provides both to the young entrepreneur and to the world at large. It doesn't require a

---

[1] http://www.bls.gov/news.release/youth.nr0.htm

specialized degree, a second mortgage, or a high-ranking title to be able to raise a CEO Kid. Likewise, becoming a CEO Kid does not require a GED, certificate, exam, or special licensing. Yet the benefits can be limitless. Let's take a brief look at just ten of them.

BENEFIT #1: ACTIVE AND MEANINGFUL EMPLOYMENT REDUCES THE RISK OF DANGEROUS AND SELF-DEFEATING ACTIVITIES.

Young people typically crave the opportunity for excelling in adult-like roles. Youth who seek but are denied access into adult-role activities often find themselves pushing the limits. Smoking, alcohol, premarital sex and pregnancy, and overall deviancy prove that adolescents will go to great lengths to achieve what they perceive to be adult status, power, and respect. Teens who have no sense of hope for successfully transitioning into adult roles often find crime as a ready substitute.

In contrast, having a sense of purpose and hope for one's future decreases the likelihood of engaging in damaging behaviors. This is why youth are often encouraged to participate in programs like the YMCA, Boy Scouts, Girl Scouts, 4-H, and Gifted Student programs. These programs bring direction, skill development, and meaningful engagement to those who participate in them.

The CEO Kids we interviewed all recognize that a sense of purpose is essential for success. That sense of purpose helps them stay focused on creating a successful life.

BENEFIT #2: PURPOSEFUL ACTIVITIES INCREASE THE LIKELIHOOD OF YOUTH MAKING HEALTHY CHOICES NOW AND IN THE FUTURE.

Not only does having a sense of purpose decrease the likelihood for making poor choices, it also increases the chances for making wise choices. Teens who have a commitment to go to college will study hard. Those who seek long-term employment will be less likely to engage in drug use. We found that CEO Kids made, and continue to make, choices that protect their business or nonprofit investment and their chances for future opportunities.

Youth learn how to make money, spend money wisely, and how to manage their time in a way that benefits their lives and the lives of their family members. They also learn more about the world than most their age, and their perspective and enjoyment for life is increased. As they learn to make decisions, they also learn to trust themselves and have confidence in their future.

BENEFIT #3: HOBBIES AND TALENTS CAN BE TURNED INTO PROFITABLE VENTURES.

Several CEO Kids (and especially their families) were surprised with how much money they could make simply by pursuing their interests and hobbies. In retrospect, it makes perfect sense that we should expect this to be the outcome; you are more likely to be successful and make money doing something you know well, are gifted in, and love doing.

As an example and part confession, years ago our son went to a yard sale where a neighbor offered to sell our son (age ten at the time) a broken-down Xbox gaming system for twenty-five cents. As parents, we explained to him that it would be a waste of his money, and it would take up too much space in his bedroom. "No problem," he persisted, "I can sell it on eBay for a profit." He smiled, and after his purchase, quietly posted it onto eBay. Within a few days, he had sold the Xbox—for $45—making more than $40 in profit after shipping and fees. "I know what it sells for," he told us with a smile. There have been many more times that he has "proved" to us that he knows his market and is capable of making profitable decisions.

Throughout this book, you'll read about dozens of other youth who, when given the opportunity (or at least the consent), have turned their hobbies, gifts, and passions into powerful income-generating machines; ones that often had huge benefits for their communities and the world. Many of these CEO Kids now have their parents and siblings working for them!

BENEFIT #4: BUILDING A BUSINESS STRENGTHENS INTERPERSONAL SKILLS AND COMMUNITY RELATIONSHIPS.

Many individuals assume that CEO Kids were born with incredible talents. In some cases, this is true. However, most had to reach beyond their comfort zones and overcome many obstacles and fears. Some were shy, fearful public speakers, or had limited social circles, and others lived in remote areas. Their passion for their businesses gave them motivation to create opportunities and pushed them into arenas that helped them grow. Networking both virtually through social media as well as in person increased their circle of influence and opened the door to engagement with mentors from around the world. Many examples of this will be cited throughout this book.

BENEFIT #5: WORKING TOWARD A GOAL STRENGTHENS THE RELATIONSHIP BETWEEN PARENT AND CEO KID.

It's difficult to fully measure how being a CEO Kid benefits family relationships, but it's clear that parents learn to trust their child more and to teach their CEO Kid important skills for success. CEO Kids often look to their parents as confidants, sources of social and financial capital, and for advice. Families become invested in seeing their CEO Kid succeed, and CEO Kids become more aware (because they see examples of families who are not invested in their youth) of how important their family connections are. Not only did we hear from many of the youth and parents that their relationships were strengthened, but we have seen the same thing in our own home. Being able to discuss business with your kids, especially when you are an entrepreneur parent, brings commonality to the relationship and helps to bridge the generational gap that often occurs between parents and tweens and teens. Whether you are riding in the car, on a vacation, or sitting at the dinner table, there is always common ground for discussion when each member of the family has a business that they are excited about.

BENEFIT #6: A BUSINESS PROVIDES A PRACTICAL FRAMEWORK FOR TEACHING CEO KIDS ABOUT FINANCIAL LITERACY AND BEHAVIOR ACCOUNTANCY.

Looking at the number of people out of work, homes in foreclosure, and the amount of consumer debt, many finance experts believe that society as a whole is clueless about financial matters. Some question whether there is accountability for individual actions in society where crime runs rampant in many areas and where there is a general attitude of entitlement. Though there are national standards for financial literacy among youth, the reality is that the implementation of those standards in public schools is rare.[2] In contrast, the CEO Kids we interviewed have learned about income, debt, expenses, investment, delayed gratification, budgeting, forecasting, and how work is involved in each of those financial aspects. We found these young entrepreneurs to be mindful of whom they are personally, and that they represent a business that, given a good image and financial stewardship, has a greater likelihood of success.

BENEFIT #7: CEO KIDS EXPERIENCE THE BENEFITS OF BEING THEIR OWN BOSS.

When people are asked why they want to be their own boss they often cite flexibility and freedom as high priorities. You can schedule your own hours, working more—or less— whenever you want. You are not confined to a schedule dictated by others.

Youth labor laws are quite strict[3] and often depend upon the type of employment and the youth's age. These laws were and are designed to protect young workers from being exploited by their employers. In many areas, young people can't even begin to work until they are at least fourteen years old. An exception to this is that children

---

[2] http://www.jumpstart.org/national-standards.html

[3] http://www.bls.gov/opub/rylf/pdf/chapter2.pdf

between the ages of seven and eighteen can be employed by their own parents who are sole proprietors. In this way, they can learn valuable skills that can help them develop their own business venture.

The labor laws do not apply, however, when you, a young entrepreneur is working for his or her self. When youth have their own business, there is much more freedom and flexibility for when, where, and how to get work done. Being able to turn gifts into profits at a young age opens the door to not only more opportunities for financial and life success, but also for gaining additional talents and traits they will need in adulthood.

BENEFIT #8: BUSINESS EXPERIENCES CREATE OPTIONS AND CHOICES.

Time and time again, those we interviewed who started out as CEO Kids and have now transitioned into adulthood told us that their experiences in their business, no matter how small, gave them opportunities and opened doors that would never have been opened otherwise. College admissions, additional employment opportunities, and networking with powerful and influential people gives CEO Kids a head start in life and provides choices that others only wish for. Those who are still kids shared experiences they have had and people that they now have connections with that will give them the critical "slight edge" as they move into adulthood. Our book clearly shows that, regardless of one's economic background, race, or residence, youth can and do succeed by following certain strategies.

BENEFIT #9: ENTREPRENEURS PROVIDE JOBS AND RESOURCES FOR THEIR COMMUNITY AND THE WORLD.

Up until this point we have looked briefly at how CEO Kids and their immediate families benefit from youth-owned businesses. However, research has shown that new businesses are a primary catalyst for economic growth.[4] This means that youth entrepreneurs can take their skills and benefit their communities in very meaningful ways. A majority of the kids we interviewed donated a portion, if not all, of their income to charity or to other social causes. Many of them were so successful that they had employees in the community or they outsourced some of the work done in the business to others; sometimes creating jobs both domestically and around the world.

BENEFIT #10: THE GROWTH CURVE IS EXPONENTIAL.

CEO Kids have experiences that dwarf that of a typical teen worker. Some of these have been briefly addressed: turning hobbies into profit (instead of using their allowance or parents' money to barely pay for their hobbies), developing leadership qualities (vs. knowing how to flip a burger 200 times each day), and being exposed to people who are genuinely concerned with their future (vs. the employer who wants them to fill a schedule). Some of the other skills CEO Kids cited learning were social media, video and audio editing, video producing, book writing, blogging, presenting on radio and TV, "pitching" to get capital for their businesses or to get clients, customer service, phone and email etiquette, and more. These skills are rarely, if ever, taught in school—and are less likely learned in more traditional youth employment outlets—but are needed in today's global workforce and economy. Our workforce and its needs are changing faster than ever, and it will require those who know how to lead. Young entrepreneurs will be at the forefront.

"From 1920 until the mid-'80s, getting a job with a large company was the dream of most every young American. The unwritten agreement between the corporation and the employee was, *if you work for us throughout your working lifetime, we will take care of you.*

---

[4] Tim Kane, "Every man (and woman) an entrepreneur". In Forbes, September 13, 2010

In the 1980s this unspoken contract disintegrated. Twenty million blue-collar workers, many of whom had spent their entire lives working for one organization, were let go. What happened? Fifty years ago, it took a lifetime for technology to make your job irrelevant—now it takes only 4 to 5 years."[5]

Most CEO Kids are four to five years *ahead* of where more traditional employment is. Their knowledge and use of business and technology will make businesses consistently dependent on them, rather than the other way around. We have witnessed in our own family, as well as in the lives of other families with CEO Kids, that small and large business in the global economy call on young entrepreneurs to do things in a way that is smarter, faster, and less expensively than before. The research we have done shows that CEO Kids not only know how to do things smarter, faster, and less expensively, but they are already learning and implementing strategies for outsourcing, sharing resources, and partnering with other CEO Kids and business leaders for mutual benefit.

The benefits of raising business-minded kids are, in reality, endless for the CEO Kids themselves, their families, the communities in which they live, and the world at large, both today and in the future. CEO Kids become powerful agents for creating great products, experiences, and services. They are agents for social good, rather than being passively molded by an ever-increasingly ineffective system. As they are empowered, they have the ability to take control of their circumstances and create bright futures for themselves and for others rather than being controlled and stifled by them.

You have just read through a list of ten benefits for raising CEO Kids. Some of them may have even inspired you to own your own business! Take a few minutes to write down your own Top 10 List of reasons and benefits for raising CEO Kids. You will want to refer back to this list and add to it as you read the rest of the book.

---

[5] Dan Miller, author of *48 Days to the Work You Love*, page 20, italics by Miller.

With so many benefits, why wouldn't more youth want to become a CEO Kid?

The Bureau of Labor Statistics indicates that less than 3% of "youth" (ages 16-24) were self-employed in July 2010.[6] In the surveys we have done both on- and off-line, we have found that most young people either don't know how to get started or they don't believe that success is possible for them—they have lost hope.

> **It is time to restore their hope! It is time to show them how to get started and give them the resources and support they need to be successful, and it starts with you!**

It's humbling to realize that, while CEO Kids are indeed extraordinary in the sense of achieving great things, they are still kids. Teens like to date and hang out with friends, many search for acceptance from their peers, and younger CEO Kids still need their mommies and daddies to bail them out every once in a while. In a way, learning about their challenges made them seem to us, well, more human. The difference between CEO Kids and many of their peers is that CEO Kids actively confront their limitations, their mishaps, and search for ways of making things better. They realize that they can make a difference, and they are engaged in doing it!

As we spent the last year researching young entrepreneurs from around the world, we were inspired to witness and remember the creativity and imagination that accompanies childhood. In our search for stories of young entrepreneurs, it has been equally discouraging to observe the annihilation of those traits as youth transition to adulthood, almost like pouring Round Up™ on the most beautiful and rare green jade flower or lady's slipper orchid simply because it doesn't match the weeds around it. Kids are often told it's not okay to be or do things differently, and that they need to color inside the lines and to march in single

---

[6] http://www.bls.gov/opub/rylf/pdf/chapter2.pdf

file. We dress them so they will "fit in" with their peers. We enroll them in clubs and organizations that the other parents in our circle of influence are enrolling their children in. We

> **As Sir Ken Robinson masterfully stated, "We're educating people out of their creative capacities."**

suppress their imaginations because there are more important things to focus on, such as reading, math, and language arts. Somehow we have come to believe that acting "childish" is wrong and they need to grow up. We restrain childhood creativity, worrying about what others will think if our child does things differently the pack. We want our children to get the "right" answers in life and in school.

It's difficult to consider what life would be like if imaginative and creative individuals had not created the telephone, the light bulb, the automobile, the Internet, or Disneyland. The exciting news is that CEO Kids retain their imagination and creativity, and use those creative capabilities as tools for their growing businesses as well as for future adventures. When we support and engage their creativity, their lives can continue to be filled with invention, imagination, spontaneity, and joy.

Throughout this book, but particularly starting with Chapter 3, you will read about a diverse group of CEO Kids who have made their dreams reality. The diversity is represented in their geography, economic situation, gender, and family background. It is also varied with respect to their income—ranging from modest profits to large fortunes—and the types of businesses they are engaged in. These CEO Kids are not only living the American Dream, they *are* the American Dream (although a few are from other parts of the world). They provide confidence to the reader and to those who apply the concepts and strategies they used to create their success.

2

The Four Pillars for Raising CEO Kids

As we interviewed hundreds of CEO Kids and their parents, we noticed that despite their differences there were common "pillars" representing their talents and experiences. Each of the pillars serves as a building block, and collectively they make up a blueprint for success. Understanding these pillars will give you and your CEO Kid the insight needed to initiate, endure, and love their business. In subsequent chapters, we'll provide more details about these pillars, examining specific attributes that make up each pillar, as well as what parents can do to foster those attributes.

Understanding the pillars will let you know what to expect, at least with some level of predictability. You won't be able to anticipate all of the challenges, or benefits, but this understanding, along with the knowledge you gain from future chapters, will give you the tools for dealing with each of them. The pillars that are involved with

> You may have the urge to skip ahead, but that would be like moving furniture into a house before the house's foundation is set!

every successful CEO Kid endeavor are *Vision, Action, Attitude,* and *Outcome.* Let's look at each of these individually.

VISION

CEO Kids have a sense of *Vision.* Vision is more than what you can see with your physical eyes. It has to do with what is envisioned or created inside the mind. Envisioning refers to knowing who you are, what you can achieve, and what is possible. It's seeing within your "minds-eye" what your purpose is, as well as putting mind pictures and emotions to dreams and goals. Envisioning often evokes all of the senses, making dreams and goals believable to the person who owns them. Having vision opens up the doors of possibility and fuels action toward goals and dreams. Individuals who have vision find that experiences and resources are provided only when they can clearly see in their mind the end result. Dr. Wayne Dyer's research in *The Power of Intention* indicates that knowing who you are and what you want to do is a source so powerful that it gives a person a way of changing the world around them.

When kids are aligned with their vision it is like "coming home" for them. They feel safe, secure, and confident in the world, and they have the courage to move forward to reach their dreams. For some CEO Kids, this feels like it was a destiny-moment, knowing that what they are doing is what they have always wanted to do and what they have wanted to become. Parents of some CEO Kids indicate that their child was always a certain way, always wanting to make a particular difference in the world, or always wanting to become a business mogul, philanthropist, or radio host. This is the case when they discover their vision early in life. Others struggle for that vision and the perfect fit for their life. They gradually come to learn what is possible in their business and gain a sense of understanding and confidence for what they are capable of personally.

Trying to start a business without a vision for the business or without your child having a sense of vision for his or her self is really a setup for failure. Vision is not only the spark for the business and for personal goals and dreams, but it is also what gives the child a sense of motivation for continuing when things get difficult. Vision serves as the first ingredient for helping your child enjoy their work despite times of long hours, challenging circumstances, and people who discourage them from following their dreams.

Justin Sachs, CEO of Justin Sachs Companies and whose business career has largely been influenced by working with Anthony Robbins at the age of sixteen, agrees that vision is the most important component for a CEO Kid.

> The most important thing I could ever tell someone is to create a vision for your life. Create a vision of what you actually want to create in your life. I even have a vision board so that it's a graphic display of exactly what I want to create in my life. It has my family, it has the house I want to move into, it has the people I want to meet, it has the things I want to do, the projects I want to create, it has a connection to my spirituality, it has a connection to everything it possibly can. How many kids I want. The car I want to drive, the whole thing. It's all on there.

Vision is a tricky thing to teach or give to your CEO Kid, and that may be one reason most children do not become CEO Kids. Parents can serve as important catalysts for vision as well as a role model of someone who possesses strong personal and business vision. However, in reality, vision cannot be directly transferred from parent to child. It's much like giving your child your own pair of glasses and asking them, "Okay, see better now?" Despite sharing genetics and a home, our children have their own interests and dislikes. Trying to force our vision for life or business on them is much like telling them to "see more clearly" by wearing our personal glasses. Being accepting of their vision, supportive of it, while keeping them grounded are parenting

16

traits that generate successful children. Justin's mother, Sheri Sachs, explains,

> We've encouraged our children to always go after their dreams, and to never have that mentality of I can't or I shouldn't. But they also need to be careful about being too unrealistic. It's important to set that goal and set the steps out on how you can reach that goal and really look forward to the end result. I think that's why Justin's has been so successful. We've never told him he couldn't do it. We've always been right there telling him that he can. I think that kind of parenting is really supportive toward the individual.

One of the more difficult moments in raising a CEO Kid can be recognizing that other people can play a larger role in instilling that vision than we can ourselves as their parents. This can be painful if we are ego driven, but if we are truly invested in our child's success we must be willing to offer them whatever skills, knowledge, or connections to others we can in order to help our children succeed. We need to swallow our pride and ask ourselves what is more important, that we get the credit for inspiring our child's success or that our child is happy in their success. In reality, we as parents also need to have a sense of vision for what it will take to help our CEO Kids succeed.

Robert Kiyosaki, author of *Rich Dad, Poor Dad,* is an excellent example of this process. Our takeaway from the book was not that one dad had lots of money and the other had nothing; instead, it was that the author was able to learn why some people are able to get ahead financially while others are not. While some people may interpret his book to mean that Mr. Kiyosaki's father was financially inept, this is not the point. The answer, we believe, is in the vision that Mr. Kiyosaki created for himself (and that was fostered by his "rich dad"). In his own words, he states, "Much of my private time was spent reflecting, asking myself questions such as 'Why does he say that?' and then asking the same of the other dad's statement. . .[it] forced me to think and ultimately choose a way of thinking for myself." [pg. 14].

Similarly, it is likely that it also gave him the opportunity to ultimately choose a way for thinking about himself. Mr. Kiyosaki's experiences gave him the vision to help himself—and to improve the financial situations of millions of households.

From our observation and research, while parents cannot force their children to have a particular vision, they usually foster and sometimes plant the seed for that *sense* of vision. That is the case for most, if not all, of the CEO Kids whom we interviewed. Indeed, many of the advances in society can be directly tied to how parents encouraged their children's sense of vision. For example, Andy Stanley explains in *Visioneering* how two boys watched their father toss an object into the air, and how the object "flew" across the room for a short time before it dropped to the ground. The object was crudely put together with a cork, bamboo, paper, screws, and rubber bands, and despite its fragileness that memory eventually led to a strong sense of vision in those two boys, whose names are well known collectively as the Wright Brothers, the pioneers of our modern airplanes.

As we explore vision in more detail, we will offer ideas, recommendations, and strategies for inspiring vision not only in your children but also in yourself.

ACTION

Wouldn't it be fabulous if merely thinking of an idea or envisioning the outcome were all that was needed to achieve and create success? The reason why vision is the first pillar, or first building block for a successful blueprint, is that action without vision is pure drudgery, and will lead to nothing of great importance. In contrast, having a sense of vision as one's foundation will make your activity much more enjoyable.

Vision gives enjoyment and commitment to one's activity because it also provides purpose for that work. CEO Kids know that their vision is the reason and purpose behind the daily or weekly tasks of balancing their budgets, marketing, selling, networking, learning about and implementing technology, and strengthening their public-speaking skills. This is a far cry from what most youth experience, as teachers can quickly attest, when their students ask, "Why do I have to know/do/learn _(fill in the blank)_ ?" Youth, as well as adults, crave a sense of purpose and reason behind what they are doing. With vision and purpose there is direction and motivation to do the work. Without it, there is complacency, unmet potential, and a sense of hopelessness.

Stevland Hardaway Judkins, born in 1950, was raised by a single-parent mother in Detroit. He experienced considerable success at an early age, hitting number one on the charts when he was thirteen, by singing and playing the bongos and harmonica, accompanied by Marvin Gaye on the drums. Stevland continued to experience success, recording dozens if not hundreds of songs revered by much of American society. While in-born talent likely had something to do with Stevland's successes, it's clear that he loved what he was doing and that he spent a lot of time working at perfecting his craft and being successful, particularly due to a disability at birth that created permanent blindness. We know Stevland better by the name of Stevie Wonder.

Many people believe that hard work will get you anywhere in life. That is only a partial truth. If it were completely true then all the people of the world who do grueling tasks and work long hours would have different outcomes for their efforts than many of them do. Vision, as remarkably demonstrated by Stevie Wonder and the Wright Brothers, is part of what brings joy to the work being done. It brings courage to embrace the opportunities that come our way and that we create out of sheer determination. When action is combined with vision, individuals can go great distances in life and businesses can grow exponentially.

Although "hard work" may include difficult labor, the true meaning of "action" encompasses so much more than toil. It also represents commitment or focus. It may also represent a lot of time spent in that laboring. Someone who is a "hard worker" is someone who goes beyond the expected requirements for a particular job, for instance.

CEO Kids are generally those who are both committed to their work and give great sums of time to taking action. They learn, or come to learn, in the words of the Chinese proverb, that "Talk doesn't cook rice." Hands-on engagement in their business and long hours are generally required for success.

Parents who teach their children how to work and to enjoy work at an early age will be more likely to help foster the beginnings of a CEO Kid. It is important when teaching principles of action, that we also teach the importance of having fun, so that we are not instilling workaholic behaviors in our kids that lead to the inability to create strong relationships now and in the future. We encourage kids to hang out with friends, to take time away from their business, and to spend time with their family.

ATTITUDE

Attitude refers to a complex interaction of how one feels about one's self, the world around them, and about one's work. It shares some commonality with vision, but vision refers to seeing what *can* be accomplished, while attitude refers to how one thinks and feels about self and circumstance, as well as *what has been (and is still to be)* accomplished.

CEO Kids generally develop a strong sense of purpose (vision) with regard to themselves and their business's potential. It is also relatively common for them to provide a great deal of work and not see things happen as they would like, at least in the short term. This is why it is quite possible, and likely, that there will be times when CEO Kids experience a positive sense of vision and a (temporary) poor attitude about themselves and the outcome of their actions. Sometimes CEO Kids will experience discouragement because their vision is so strong and/or high reaching that they have failed to see the possible pitfalls and bumps along the journey. When they reach those pitfalls and bumps, the discouragement is harder to take because there is no forewarning for them. The CEO Kids may feel discouraged by the letdown as well as the embarrassment of not being prepared for the possibility of what they perceive as failure.

Young people have a great deal of imagination and creativity, which are key pieces in the success of a business start-up, but they have less life experience in dealing with disappointments, especially financially. This is where parents of CEO Kids are so important. Parents have the life experiences to console and encourage their CEO Kids to keep going, to keep things in perspective, and to feel good about themselves and their business despite temporary setbacks.

A popular saying is that "Attitude determines altitude," and that definitely applies to CEO Kids. Having positive feelings about who they are and what they do greatly determines how far they will go with their business. Perhaps one of the best stories on the intersection between vision, action, and attitude is that of Abraham Lincoln. As a child, Abraham Lincoln lost his mother to sickness when he was nine years old. Fortunately for him, his father remarried and he had a strong relationship with the woman he then called "mother."

However, he grew quite distant from his father and disliked the hard work of prairie life (his father called Abe "lazy"). The story could have ended quite badly and for good reasons. Sociological scholars would point to the loss of the parent, the poor relationship with the father, the lack of education, and the bad fit between the child and his environment as indicators of psychological risk for Abe. Fortunately, that is not where the story ends.

As a young adult, Abe's life adventures attest to his belief in himself and what he could accomplish (vision). He worked hard, studying and applying his knowledge (action), and his legendary attitude despite difficulties created a man who faced hardship, war, and political accusations. What is so incredible about Lincoln is that he was able to foster a sense of all three pillars into the others: vision ("all are created equal"), action (in major political, law, and war decisions), and attitude (feeling that despite hardship and division as a nation, we needed to keep going). The

Gettysburg Address is an excellent example of his mastery over the three pillars.

OUTCOME

CEO Kids are goal-oriented. Their vision is to change something (e.g., income, situation, themselves), and they usually work hard to achieve their preferred outcome. As parents, it is important to help CEO Kids understand that the outcome is sometimes found in small increments of change, as there is often a false understanding that "small results" at various stages equals failure. Even when CEO Kids have a positive attitude, things are generally not going to be transformed overnight. Parents must be there to support, encourage, and guide their CEO Kids in a way that helps them see each outcome, no matter how small, as success and important in creating the fulfillment of vision, rather than only focusing on the final outcome.

Sometimes the pillars will need rebalancing. If a CEO Kid does not meet his or her goals or desired vision, it may mean more action or *smarter* action is needed. It may mean that attitude and belief need to improve. It may also require a change in vision, which, as noted, is often evolving as CEO Kids gain more experience. Revising one's vision isn't a bad thing; it may be a necessary outcome that leads to even better results than were previously envisioned. When vision, action, and attitude align properly, then one can expect awesome outcomes.

SUMMARY OF THE PILLARS

It is imperative that vision be the first pillar that CEO Kids develop, in order for things to progress smoothly in their business. Recognizing what one wants to be, do, and have—even if the vision later evolves—is important to not only motivate one to work, but to work smarter, more focused, and, yes, sometimes longer. Action, by itself, may not lead to the results CEO Kids would like, at least as quickly as they would like. That is why it is important for them to develop a proper attitude toward what they have already done and toward what they will be and do in the future. CEO Kids are often naturally goal-oriented, but helping your child put things into context by encouraging him or her to recognize smaller successes or positive outcomes will help your CEO Kid overcome difficult times and improve their business. As we go through this book, you will see that these attributes are more interconnected than distinctly different from one another, but it is a good idea to separate them when considering them for the first time.

QUESTIONS FOR REFLECTION

Taking time to answer these questions will allow you to assess where you are personally in life as well as where your kids are. Encourage them to take time to answer the questions for themselves. Once you know where you are, you can make a plan to keep going or chart a new course for the life you dream of and desire.

1. Where do you see yourself with regards to vision for yourself and your life work? Where do you see yourself in one year, five years, and ten years?
2. Where do you see that each of your children is with the vision they have for themselves and for their future?
3. How do you view work and taking action?
4. Do you love the work that you currently do?
5. What skills or gifts that you possess and love could you turn into income that you are not currently monetizing?
6. What skills or gifts do your children possess that they could turn into income?
7. How is your attitude in regards to self, life, and your work?
8. What is the attitude of each of your children? Is it a reflection of your attitude?
9. Are you getting the outcomes that you want from what you are putting into life?
10. Are your children getting the outcomes that they want from what they are putting into life?

11. If the answer to #9 and #10 is No, what do you think would need to change?
    a. Vision
    b. Action
    c. Attitude
    d. All of the above

3

CEO Kid Pillar #1: VISION

Thus far we have looked at some generalities about the four CEO Kids' pillars: Vision, Action, Attitude, and Outcome. Now that a foundation for the basics has been given, we can consider each of these pillars with greater specificity and application, using information provided directly from CEO Kids themselves.

Each pillar is representative of particular characteristics that CEO Kids have told us are very useful to them. This chapter and the next few chapters will address these characteristics commonly referred to as "attributes." These are the attributes that CEO Kids have used to grow their business, endure difficulties, and thrive as individuals. We focus on youth and former youth entrepreneurs to show both a snapshot and progression of their experiences. Within each of the four pillar-based chapters, you will also learn from parents who have "been there" and have successfully raised CEO Kids.

Earlier we talked about vision, and its relevance to the other pillars. Vision's characteristics or attributes consist of having a sense of purpose for yourself and your business, and feeling driven to succeed or accomplish your goals. Let's take a look at some of these characteristics in CEO Kids and how to foster those characteristics.

PURPOSE

If you have ever worked a job or lived a portion of your life without purpose, you know how important purpose is. Without purpose, time drags, hope dwindles, and commitment fails. People without purpose often have lives filled with depression, anxiety, and health issues. In contrast, having a sense of purpose gives direction, hope, and serves as the foundation for one's commitment to achieve. The CEO Kids who are most passionate about their business and life have a sense of purpose for who they are and what they can become or do in life. For some, like Jason Kirby, who owns The Right Light Photography, the purpose for their business is to be in control of their own lives. Jason said,

> I don't want to follow the same path of being stuck to an employer, having to depend on that monthly paycheck that any time especially during this economy, they can pull that away from you. I want to be in control of my own destiny. So that was probably the biggest motivator that got me started.

A sense of purpose can evolve from many sources. It can come from a lifelong goal, a moment in time, or because of heartache. For some, like Chelsea Eubank, owner of Faithful Fish, a sense of purpose provides resiliency to get through difficult times.

It's incredible when young entrepreneurs can transform tragedy into triumph and turn what appears to be a mess into a message of hope and life. Nashely Ruiz started her non-profit organization after her grandmother died, and named it after her grandmother. It's called PEPPA, which stands for People Educating People on Poverty Awareness.

I've always been in love with the clothing and fashion industry. When I was sixteen, I lost three family members, including my dad. It led me to a place where I wanted to renew my faith, or to be able to wear my faith on my sleeve. I drew up some designs and my mom liked them, and then I considered the bigger picture about starting a business.

Another example of success from tragedy comes from Jordan Puchinger of Silver Jax, who started his business after a car accident.

I started my first *real* business when I was 15 years old. I was in a rather serious car accident. After leaving the hospital, I had a few spare months that left me really just lounging or in bed, which ultimately left me behind the computer. Shortly after I returned to school, I competed in Skills Canada for web design and web development. I won locals, provincials, and then represented Alberta in Halifax, Nova Scotia, and placed very high.

Purpose is part of one's vision; it is the reason for what you are doing. That purpose, or a sense of why, is what motivates you to action. It doesn't take an accident or tragedy to bring out that vision in most people, but our point, as authors, is to help you see that if even those who are experiencing tragedy can succeed, then so can you! Do not let your current circumstances dictate or determine the life you wish to live or the success you create for yourself.

There is an inescapable reality that a child's sense of purpose will rarely survive if their parents are critical of that sense of purpose. However, ironically, as parents, we often fail to recognize ourselves being critical of our children's dreams or goals. It tends to be clothed or camouflaged with good intensions, such as wanting to protect our child from pain or disappointment, or by giving "constructive" feedback. Chelsea Eubank's mom, Linda, explains the challenge of balancing protection and acceptance of children: "As parents, we all tend to focus [too much] on what they struggle with and not focus on what they're good it."

Elaine, mother of CEO Kid Lexxi Saal, thirteen, founder of LexxiLoves.org, an organization that provides funds to foster care and those less fortunate during the

> Children haven't been jaded like adults have. They think they can conquer the world, and believe they can accomplish anything. Believe in them, even when they are small. . . it's very important.

holidays, adds this advice:

How do we know when we have crossed the line in being critical rather than serving as a supportive guide for our child? Look at the outcome. When a child feels *en-*Couraged, we've done things right. When a child feels *dis-*Couraged, it is often the result of criticism.

The counter to criticism is acceptance. True acceptance of your child will often require leaving some of the overprotection and ego that comes along with it behind.

> "Never tell them they cannot do something. Put forward a couple of alternative suggestions and let them think about it and come to their own conclusions." — Jacqui Haggerty, mother of Steven Haggerty, creator of *Salut World*.

Clark Hodges, father of youth entrepreneur and iPhone App creator Freddie Anne Hodges, further adds, "Our children probably won't recognize the benefit for years down the road, but you'll probably give them confidence that they can achieve and do things on their own."

Our own bias, and one that is shared by others, is that parents should not try to instill their own dreams or sense of purpose for a business into their child. Children have their own dreams and goals, and borrowing from their parents' purpose (rather via business or other life endeavors) will only get them so far. Holding on to the parents' dreams can prove damaging for the child if they never learn to dream themselves or to find their own purpose. It can also be damaging for the parent-child relationship if the child is holding on to those dreams out of fear of rejection or disapproval from the parent(s). The key is to encourage, support, and accept children and youth, and provide opportunities in a way that gives your child confidence, experience, skills, and wings to soar.

Zhu Shen, mother of Perry Chen, award-winning movie critic, knows this better than most people. She said,

> Two years ago when we first started, I had no plan or specific goal about being nationally known—none of that. It was just my desire to challenge him, and have him be writing, and enjoy the reading part. I think when we first started, he was only reviewing DVDs that we already owned. Then we had a wonderful teacher of his who worked well with him and with me, and who agreed with me that Perry could write reviews.

Zhu accepted the gift that Perry has, and worked with another influential adult in Perry's life to help him foster the talent he already had. They weren't changing him into being or doing something he didn't like or want to do—they were building what was already there. That is how you can foster a sense of purpose and vision in your own child. Build on the gifts and talents that they already have and that they find joy in using.

A sense of purpose is unique to each individual. Of all the young entrepreneurs we interviewed, we found that most of their businesses evolved out of an interest or hobby that they were passionate about. We encourage youth and their families to take the time to build the foundation of purpose before trying to begin a business. We also recommend that you do research as to whether a business is "market ready", because there are cases where basing a business on pure personal passion can mean a recipe for disaster and a huge amount of debt. Encourage your kids to create a business that not only satisfies their passion, but also has the potential for profit. It may take a few tries and a bit of time and investigation, but it is totally worth the effort and the money saved from not investing in something that won't work.

QUESTIONS FOR REFLECTION

1. What experiences, tragedies, successes, or life circumstances do you have that you could redirect into a purpose and mission for life and business?
2. What experiences, tragedies, successes, or life circumstances have your children had that they could redirect into a purpose and mission for life and business?

DRIVE

Many CEO Kids feel driven to achieve, succeed, create, or prove a point that their idea is possible. For some, this feeling stems from a belief that their accomplishments or experiences were made just for them; that they were born to achieve the vision they have. Feeling driven occurs when one's interests and talents align with the right opportunity.

As a teen, Anshul Samar said he "always wanted to be a CEO." He definitely had a vision to be a leader. Anshul's talent was understanding chemistry, but he was also quite interested in games. When he asked his parents to play games with him, they'd often tell him "no" because the games didn't have any educational value. That gave Anshul an idea, and that idea provided the intersection where interest, talents, and opportunity came together—Anshul created a fun and educational game (to learn chemistry) called "Elementeo."

Mary Sarah Gross, at the age of twelve, learned of an audition for KidzBop[7] and told us it was "definitely" something she wanted to do. Although the audition was successful, Mary Sarah's mother, Patricia, seemed reluctant because there was a heavy price or investment if they wanted to pursue Mary Sarah's youthful career. The pursuit of her dreams meant Mary Sarah and Patricia would be by riding a bus "on tour" for a whole year. After family discussions and prayer, the family decided to support Mary Sarah. They did the KidzBop tour and the rest is history. Mary Sarah has gone on to become a professional singer.

When she was twelve years old, Becca Robison, founder of Astrotots.org, had the vision of going into space. Unfortunately, the community response to that vision was poor, and at times led to people telling her that she could never reach her dream because of her gender. Her vision and purpose expanded to wanting to help other girls believe they can achieve space travel. Her company, AstroTots, provides girls with both the knowledge and, in particular, confidence

---

[7] http://www.kidzbop.com/music

in themselves so that they can achieve their dreams. Becca's vision was so real to her that it drove her ability to accomplish great things for herself and for others. Belief in oneself was echoed frequently by several of the youth entrepreneurs.

Another young entrepreneur who exemplifies "drive" is Dale Stephens, who initiated several businesses throughout his childhood, including a flower delivery and photography business. At the age of eighteen, he is starting his own airline and has recently created an organization, Un-College, that serves as an alternative to the current educational system.

Some parents we spoke with found that "drive" was often facilitated into tangible results as they listened to their child, helped brainstorm, and offered encouragement. For example, our daughter Clarissa loves to cook but was having a hard time seeing how she could make money cooking when she was only eleven, she didn't have access to a commercial kitchen, and there is so much red tape involved with making and selling food. Her vision of selling her specialty granola or cookies seemed dashed. As we began brainstorming with her the possibilities of ways she could turn her gifts and interests into income, pictures and visions of other possibilities began to form in her head. She organized a charity bake sale, wrote a cookbook, started a blog, and has raised hundreds of dollars for kids with cancer.

QUESTIONS FOR REFLECTION
1. What is your child most passionate about?
2. What motivates your child to succeed?
3. How can you help turn your child's "drive" into positive outcomes?

LOOKING FOR A UNIQUE SYSTEM FOR EMPOWERING YOUTH?

Scan the QR code below or go to page 207 to find out what it says.

GOALS

Having a sense of purpose and drive for one's business are vital attributes, but it's also very important to set goals. Having purpose and drive without goals is a little like wanting to drive across the country and having your foot on the pedal, but not knowing which direction is the right way to get to where you want to go. Robert Van Hoesel, seventeen, of Robert Van Hoesel Design, creates websites and believes that "the most important thing in being successful is to make goals in order to make progress."

In our interviews and visits with CEO Kids and their parents, we have found that parents have a powerful influence with regard to goal formation, and often help clarify goals of their youth entrepreneurs. Believing in your child is one of the best gifts you can give, not only with entrepreneurship but also in life.

When kids come to you as a parent, first listen to what they are saying. Ask questions to gain clarification. Before offering any suggestions, ask them if they would like a suggestion or recommendation. Getting their permission to offer a suggestion or give a recommendation helps them to know you are validating who they are, and it allows them to be in control of their idea and how they would like the development of it handled.

As you move through conversations with your children in clarifying their goals and decisions, be sure to always let them know that you support who they are and that you will be there for them no matter what the outcome. This leads to an improved sense of confidence.

QUESTIONS FOR REFLECTION

1. Why do you think a sense of purpose and drive influence the goals children make for themselves?
2. How can you, as a parent or mentor, help your young entrepreneur clarify his or her goals?
3. In what ways can you ensure that you are supporting, rather than dictating, your child's goals?

ARE YOU A CEO KID OR DO YOU KNOW A CEO KID?

Scan the QR code below or go to page 207 to find out what it says

4

CEO KID PILLAR #2: ACTION

In the novel *Holes* by Louis Sachar, a boy (Stanley Yelnats) is sent to a reform camp for a crime he didn't commit. His sentence is to dig holes in the desert because, as he is told, digging holes builds character. Perhaps the reason the book (and the movie) is so inspiring is due to the human folly that it addresses: society's belief that hard work—one of drudgery—is a virtue. In actuality, the opposite is true: Without vision (or purpose), working hard will only breed contempt and disdain for the work being done.

Young entrepreneur Joe Meglio, owner of Meglio Fitness, explained how important it was for him and others to build upon one's vision for youth entrepreneurship.

> I really believe you need to have a vision of where you want your business to go. When opening up a business, there are no guarantees, and there will never be a perfect time to start it up. However, if you have a vision of what you want to accomplish, you need to *take action*.

Parents and mentors are very important when it comes to Action. Youth often have grand ideas, but they also frequently struggle with recognizing how much effort it will take to reach their goals. Parents can foster their child's sense of purpose by helping their child recognize how the action is possible and that it will lead to the desired outcome.

Both parents and kids should identify role models and mentors they want to learn from, be around, or emulate. Chris Spradlin, founder of Epic Parent TV and father of youth entrepreneur Cole Spradlin, owner of Grassman Lawncare in Colorado, said,

> Mentors play a significant role in our parenting and raising our kids. Jodie and I are very strategic about the people/adults that we surround our kids with. I have a plan that when Cole turns 13, he will spend time with certain business owners by going to work with them and learning more about the business world.

In this chapter we'll look at some of the more common and most successful elements that CEO Kids use while working, and we'll gain a better understanding of how parents can foster those characteristics in their children. Action is indeed a work in progress, and the characteristics that best assist the CEO Kid are understanding (1) that knowledge is cumulative, and (2) how to best utilize networking.

Parents are often also involved in the work process. Consider Kim Braboy, mother of Hannah Braboy of Hannah Braboy Photography, who says,

> Along the way, we have purchased some major equipment (before she had a way to pay for it herself), furnished transportation, and acted as business advisors for her to bounce ideas off of. We have also home schooled since Hannah was in third grade, giving her maximum time to pursue her interests.

CUMULATIVE LEARNING

Erik Erikson, the author of the *Psychosocial Theory*, which addresses both inherent drive and social responses, maintained that life is a process of collecting information, attitudes, and experiences that, with each new stage of life, are built upon. The premise is that success builds subsequent success. The theory, or at least that premise, fits perfectly with the CEO Kids—and many of their parents—that we interviewed. In nearly every CEO Kid, there was the recognition that their business grew from their earlier experiences and knowledge. Here are a few examples of cumulative learning in action and advice from successful youth entrepreneurs.

Leanna Archer, who owns and runs Leanna's Inc., a body and hair care company, recommends reading all you can about the business you want to form.

> First of all, find out what exactly you want to do in starting a company. What do you want to market, or what kind of industry are you interested in entering? Learn everything you can about it. That's one of the advantages that we have having the internet and technology.

Austin Evers, sixteen, creator of Appuous, Inc., continues with the explanation that cumulative learning is essential when working to best understand what product or service would lead to success.

> I definitely spent a fair amount of time researching the industry. I answered some fundamental questions when researching, such as: Who are my potential customers? How many apps are out there? What is the most popular app and what can I pull from the success of that app and implement it into my own? What is the average price of an app? What is the category breakdown of all the apps?

This love for lifelong learning is critical for success, whether it is youth entrepreneurship or life in general. Parents who help instill in their children that learning is more than just going to school—that it takes place anywhere and everywhere—and that learning is rewarding, tend to find that their children enjoy learning.

Shama Kabani Hyder, founder and CEO of The Marketing Zen Group, said this of her parents' engagement in learning and education:

> They instilled a love of learning in me that has driven everything I've done. For us, a book was a treat. It wasn't a thing we had to do; we loved it. Learning is not school or books but it goes beyond, and you can learn from everyone and every experience, and that was very valuable to me.

Dallas Goodwin is just nine years old and successfully sells jewelry and other accessories. She is articulate and wise beyond her years, offering the following advice for youth entrepreneurs: "Get good at one of the things you're doing first and then branch out—add more things later. Get really good at one thing before you keep moving to other things."

Ben Lang started selling on eBay years ago and is now a pro-blogger while being a student. Over the years, he learned how to effectively use technology and started promoting his business using Twitter, LinkedIn, and YouTube. He created so much success he was interviewed on TV and now blogs about entrepreneurship, technology, and social media. Ben has over 11,000 followers on Twitter. One of the tips Ben shared is to "keep your resume current because the experiences and skills will often pile on fast!" A young entrepreneur's successes may be hard to keep track of (for resumes or college applications) if you don't keep up with their documentation.

With regards to continuous learning and implementing change, Shane Hudson, founder of the Success Circuit blog, says:

> If I didn't do things differently, then I don't know if I would be where I am now. My last blog was not very successful and I did give up with it actually. I learned so much from that experience though that Success Circuit would not be here if it wasn't for that.

Matt Hackney, twenty-seven, started his business experience when he was thirteen by designing computer systems for hospitals. He has continued to use his talents and has created a business of multiple trades: model, author, actor, dance instructor, publisher, and more. Matt believes that "progression—not perfection—is the best outlook on things. It doesn't have to be perfect the first time, and you'll set yourself up for failure if you don't have that outlook."

Matt's comments illustrate what many CEO Kids learn: It's okay to fall or make mistakes as long as you learn from them. We write more about this mindset in the next chapter.

Particularly among very young entrepreneurs, we found that many parents are concerned about balancing the marketing of the business and protecting the child from dangerous outside forces. While marketing and promoting the business is key to the success of the business, you'll first want to know your own comfort level [with others seeing your child's picture on the Internet, giving your home address, school information, phone number, etc.]. There are ways to protect young entrepreneurs while growing a business. Some parents have chosen to open a post office box rather than provide the home address of their youth entrepreneur.

Nancy O'Neill, mother of Jason O'Neill, the founder of Pencil Bugs, had this to say about protecting her son while encouraging him to accumulate knowledge and experience and create business success:

> The only real thing I was concerned about in the beginning was his safety and security. When we put the website up, I didn't put our address on there, I was very careful about what personal information we added. Posting his picture in the beginning was like, Oh no, am I doing the right thing? Little things like that. We closely monitor all his business activity. I wasn't all that concerned once we got the business set up and everything was legitimate and things were going okay, there wasn't a way for someone to contact him in an inappropriate manner. I was always here and seeing what was going on.

Another piece of knowledge that's gained over time is financial literacy. Understanding a balance sheet, expenses, cash flow, and profit is important in order to determine how viable the business is, how much the CEO Kid (or the family) is investing in it, and where the money is going. Many CEO

Kids are initially surprised to see how much they are truly making—and spending.

There are several financial programs available to monitor a business's income and expenses, and many of them are free. Some examples are listed in the back of this book. It's a good idea to try a few before you decide on one. Whatever the system you choose to manage the money, we recommend requiring your CEO Kid to be part of the process. You want the system to be easy enough to use that they can learn to understand it and run it themselves with some guidance from you. Even a simple ledger (such as a notebook with columns) can serve as a visible reminder as to what is going on financially with the business. Keeping track of their business and personal finances is a trait that will improve their lives, especially as they grow into adults. If you cannot teach them these principals, find someone or some program that can. In the back of the book are many resources that can help you teach your kids about finance as well as help manage the business income and expenses.

CEO Kids benefit greatly when homes are the school for financial literacy and where financial accountability is taught naturally. Derek Johnson, founder of Tatango, shared with us his experience with financial accountability while he was growing up:

> My parents always ran our family like a business. If we wanted to be reimbursed for a movie ticket or something, we had to submit a receipt or an expense report or a bill. This kind of showed my sister and me how business worked from a very young age.

A final item of cumulative learning involves understanding what the market is for the product or service of the business. Nick Ferguson, an accomplished cyclist and owner of Sustained Fitness in Australia, offers some great advice on this.

I think the most important part of marketing was understanding what I do. I still develop that as I go, but I had so many areas where I wanted to help people I needed to focus a little. I'm looking to work with people who are driven and motivated, who have the resources to get there.

QUESTIONS FOR REFLECTION
1. How can you encourage your kids to embrace cumulative learning?
2. What skills do they already have that they could build upon and turn into a business or nonprofit?
3. Where could they go or what could they do to further their education in the area that they are most interested in turning into a business or nonprofit?

NETWORKING

Young entrepreneur and online marketer David King said it best when he said,

> I think one of the most profitable areas of businesses is networking, just to build your network and grow your network, and grow from each other is a huge asset to any business owner.

A network can be made up of members of online communities, sports teams, churches, schools, or even people in a neighborhood. For example, Drew DeLeon, owner of AktiveWrap, networks with schools and sports teams to promote fundraising efforts while selling her product.

One of the more common gifts that parents give their CEO Kids is the understanding of networking. Youth are sometimes better at online social networking, and with technology as a whole, than their parents, but parents often serve as relational capital for their children when networking with adults online and in person. Both online and face-to-face networking are vital components of a successful business. Many parents we interviewed took their kids to networking events such as Chamber of Commerce luncheons, TweetUps, and MeetUps. A large number also took them along to business conferences, where the kids were able to learn alongside their parents as well as meet adult business leaders.

Being willing to ask people for advice is perhaps one of the biggest benefits of networking. Jessica Cervantes started her entrepreneurial journey when she was twelve. She is the founder and CEO of Popsy Cakes and says this of her experiences with asking adults and professionals for advice and help:

When I first started my business, I just started sending emails asking people if they can help me. A lot of people wouldn't do that because they'd think nobody would help them, but you'd be surprised with all the big-time entrepreneurs who would help you. I actually filed a patent, and when I shared my business idea with patent lawyers they decided to do it pro bono—instead of a $20,000 cost—just because I sent them an email.

Young entrepreneur Ryan Coisson, who has developed several businesses, also believes that, in addition to more traditional networking, reading provides a great deal of advice or access to mentors "by proxy". He says, "I've always believed in investing in myself, whether that be through books, time with people, or even having a coach or something like that."

Similarly, parents can help their youth understand the importance of networking *outside* of the online arena. Let's look at a few examples of how parents and other adults can help youth network.

Anshul Samar, creator of Elementeo, was driven to different conferences to "get the word out" about his game. At one of the conferences he was given a free booth, and a mentor there gave Anshul the stage and microphone to promote his game. A video of that speech went viral, and it led to interviews with many different media outlets and interviews.

Lane Sutton, The Kid Critic and social media consultant, encourages youth entrepreneurs to network by passing out their own business cards that include a call to action or perhaps with a coupon or coupon code.

It's important to realize that networking isn't only for the purpose of building clients, but can also be for emotional and content support. For example, Jayson Kingsbeer, youth entrepreneur and founder of Jason Kingsbeer Photography, states the following, when asked what he would recommend for other youth entrepreneurs:

> What's really helped me in my business is that I have surrounded myself with other photographers. I've talked to some really amazing photographers, award-winning photographers, all over the world. If I have something go wrong in my business, I just ask and they help me because they've had years of experience.

We can see from these experiences that networking, as well as how parents assist with that networking, varies considerably based upon the needs of the business and abilities of the young entrepreneurs. Some, because of their age or where social confidence is not yet formed, will need more help from their parents with networking. Others will simply need parents to play chauffeur to the places they need to go to network.

As authors and parents, we (especially Sarah) have been active in helping our children network in a way that facilitates their business, their skills, and opens doors for future opportunities. For example, we have chauffeured our son Jacob, owner of Jake's Tutorials and Tech Support, to places where he can fix people's computers as well as to TweetUps and MeetUps. We have also networked with individuals in a way that helped our daughter, Clarissa, owner of Creating with CC, get her cookbook published. We are also using our current network to help our eight-year-old son Jonathan (aka "Jumpin' Jack Jon"), build a group of resources and experts in his quest for developing a review channel on YouTube and a physical fitness program for young kids.

When trying to contact new people or trying to sell an idea, product, or service to someone for the first time, it's important to make sure to have all your facts straight, a great script, and have done plenty of practicing. It wouldn't hurt to have a brief mission statement (or "Purpose") for the business, along with four or five main goals of that business. Those goals, or values, must be sincere and ones that clearly drive the business, as well as strengthen the ties of existing customers or clients.

It's one thing to have a presentation ready for people, but it's another to "own" that presentation. Whether your CEO Kid is selling online, at a booth, or elsewhere, they will be tested by prospective clients to make sure they are capable and "know their stuff". We recommend that your CEO Kid practice their sales speech (or introduction of themselves and their business) several times in front of a parent. The idea is that if your CEO Kid can give a successful speech in front of a parent (whom they often see as a "corrector"), then they can give it to anyone. Derek Johnson, owner of Tatango, provides a glimpse of his plan for presenting his business to others. "I did my [sales] speech 100–200 times before I ever presented to anyone. If you can go up there and do it without note cards or without using your slides you will impress people."

Ethan Thompson of Just Passing Through Media, encourages young entrepreneurs to read as much as possible so that they feel comfortable talking with a diverse group of individuals, and to show potential clients that they are knowledgeable, which generates respect and trust.

Customer service is another valued component of networking and return business, as well as referrals. Ben Johnson, youth entrepreneur and founder of Running Wild Paintball, is fortunate to have learned these skills and values from an early age.

> You have to be able to talk to people, and [have] a level head. There's always something that doesn't go exactly right or according to plan, and you've got to solve the problem. If you give the customer enough time and attention, they'll come back, or they'll tell others "they've got a nice place—they're nice people."

Similarly, Lane Sutton, The Kid Critic, advised:

> Ask yourself: why should they follow you? What would your followers want? Maybe they want a coupon. Maybe some great resources. Find amazing people and retweet them. People like that.

John Naylor, founder of John Naylor Landscapes and Lawn Care, started his business when he was very young and believes that honesty literally pays off.

> Clients and customers expect honesty and hard work in return for a payment. I think that's critical to treat your clients well and again that's going to pay you back because they're going to recommend you to their friends and family and neighbors and all that.

In many cases, parents can serve as a bridge between the youth entrepreneur and those who are older than them. Teens may have different interests, talents, and needs than other generations, and parents can help their teens recognize how their skills can improve life for several generations. For example, our son Jacob is able to fix computers for people who were not raised in the technological age. He has the patience to explain to them what needs to be fixed rather than just charging them a huge price to fix it, like some of his competitors do. Lane Sutton is able to do something similar by acting as a consultant and social media manager for solopreneurs and companies owned by people who are much older than he is but who do not have a strong understanding of social media and how to use it to grow business.

When it comes to cumulative learning, parents need to decide how far they are willing to go to support their child's learning and progress. Many parents offer some level of capital, often in the form of a loan, a computer or other equipment, chauffeuring, time, and a huge range of assistance from customer service to securing media coverage. Some parents are determined to give "their all" in exchange for the well-being of their child. Allyson Ames, owner of Wonderland Bakery, had this to say about her mom, Sondra Ames:

> My mom was always committed to what I wanted to do...and during this conversation, I turned the question to her: If we lost our home what would she do? She told me that a house does not bring you happiness and that she could live anywhere. Helping me create and realize my dream and working apron to apron with me would be the most amazing experience and she was fully committed. Failure was not an option and we could change the world one cookie and cupcake at a time.

Another example of a parent who has given her all is Jason O'Neill's mom, Nancy. Jason has been in business since he was nine years old and Nancy has spent countless hours designing and updating his website, securing and monitoring media coverage, editing his book, speech writing, chauffeuring, helping to manage his social media outlets, and so much more. Jason has had an incredible amount of cumulative learning in the last six years, and his mom has been there every step of the way.

QUESTIONS FOR REFLECTION
1. Who do you know that you could introduce to your young entrepreneur as a mentor, potential client, or investor?
2. What organizations, TweetUps, or events are available for you to take your CEO Kid to in order to introduce them to people and teach them networking and public speaking skills?

3. Do you have social media accounts and are you actively using them to engage in relationships that could potentially be of benefit to your CEO Kid?
4. Think of 5 ways that you could cultivate relationships right now that will be of mutual benefit now or in the future.

5

CEO KID PILLAR #3: ATTITUDE

C EO Kids are most often highly ambitious youth. This is generally a positive trait, but the difficult thing for them to remember is that they are kids—and they need to experience a kid life—in order to stay balanced. The more successful they are, the more important it is to remember to keep that balance. (This is true for adults, also).

BALANCE

Parents and adult leaders can help youth maintain the "balance" needed through many different avenues. The first is by doing what parents do best—protect them. Earlier in this book, we learned how we, as parents, can be overprotective and, as a result, keep children from accomplishing their vision.

> We always tried to encourage and support Joe in his endeavors, but always reminded him to keep his priorities and values in order. To keep balance, always do in life what you enjoy doing and what you believe in." —Lucy Meglio, mother of Joe Meglio of Meglio Fitness

Melissa Rose, founder of Biz in the Boxx and mother of youth entrepreneur Sydney Powell, said,

> Don't make them dread working on their business because you have too much of a hand involved in it. Kids have amazing ideas and clarity and we tend to underestimate their abilities. They see things far differently than adults do.

But the opposite can also be true, where youth entrepreneurs can become so absorbed in their work that their friendships can slip and their enjoyment with life in general can suffer.

Fifteen-year-old Dakota Lee, author of *Flash of Freedom,* said,

> Don't become too serious. No matter how you look at your business, you are still a kid. You can't grow up too fast. For a while there, for quite a few months, I was growing up way too fast. All of a sudden, I couldn't fit in with my peers. . . [then] I couldn't keep up with the business because that wasn't who I was. Make sure you have time for yourself for a kid. Put down time on the calendar where you can be yourself.

That is great advice for anyone who is overly ambitious. Whether you are a CEO Kid or an adult, learning to take time away from the business is so important.

Craig Sutton, father of Lane Sutton, The Kid Critic, provides the following advice:

It's always a work in progress. It's a passion but we have to try and balance [life]. Because he is still young, we try to protect him from the world wide Web (because so much of Lane's business is online). Lane sees the pressures, the successes, the fun part—the one thing we always try to help Lane with is balance by not always having to be serious all time—but to have fun too. Let life blossom, and not focus on just one thing.

Andy Garbera, father of David Garbera, founder of KH Smilers, explains that balance is partially maintained by not creating pressure for their son in his business. "The biggest challenge is maintaining a balance, and we did not push Dave in any way."

Jason Kingsbeer, of Jason Kingsbeer Photography, likes to make sure he focuses heavily on completing his schoolwork Monday through Friday, so that he can focus on photographing weddings (or hanging out with his friends) on the weekends.

Zhu Shen, mother of Perry Chen of *Perry's Previews,* said, "I have the challenge to help him to still enjoy his childhood, getting to do some fun things outside of school and movie critique role, by going to the zoo and nature walks regularly on the weekends."

Johnna, mother of Ben Johnson, of Running Wild Paintball, said, "He plays three sports, and we really want him to experience his childhood, too. We don't want it to be a drag for him; he goes on sporting events and dates and everything."

Deborah Onderdonk, mother of young entrepreneur Ryan Coisson, also let us know that encouragement toward life is really the same thing as encouraging their son in his work. "I told him that he should find something he loved to do and make that his life's work. We encouraged him to look at life as an adventure."

Savannah Ross, mother of Ryan Ross, The Tiny Trump, told us,

> Ryan's been interviewed by a multitude of television programs and magazines and newspapers throughout the world. And I think as parents, you really want to protect them from what's out there. You've got to have that balance between allowing him to prosper in his business and allowing him to build in confidence and to get the recognition he deserves, but we also need to keep him safe and grounded and make sure that he's not being exploited. I find it can easily go that direction.

There are times when business and life may get out of balance. Steven Gordon of Tattoo ID shares that he has "sacrificed a lot of sleep, and prepared in advance. Going out on weekends is rare because I do all of my homework and cut the tattoos. Luckily, I have friends who understand. When me and my best friend Gary hang out, we usually end up working anyway."

Help your CEO Kid remember how important friendships are, and that taking "breaks" are vital to the health of their bodies, minds, and businesses. Helping young entrepreneurs deflect stress will also strengthen their trust in you and in the advice you will give them in the future.

Of course, it's easy for parents to become absorbed in the business also. Michelle Bennett, mother of Olivia Bennett, artist extraordinaire, found that her daughter had a talent and recognized that there are more important things in life than household chores. To keep "balance" as a parent, you must first identify what your priorities are. "You can think to yourself, Oh my gosh, I've neglected this or I've forgotten that. And you can't beat yourself up about it, but you can definitely spend one-on-one time with the other kids. I try to do that and make them feel special because that's very important."

QUESTIONS FOR REFLECTION

1. Are there areas of your personal life or your CEO Kid's life that needs more balance?
2. What are three steps you can take to create more fun, and enjoyment in your life, and in your child's life?
3. Do you need to set boundaries on time investment areas of your life so that you and your kids can learn to "step away" from the stress and demand for constant achievement?

CHARITY

Staying balanced as a CEO Kid means more than just having fun; it's more of a mindset than anything else. Being grateful and wanting to "give back" to charity is one of the most powerful methods we know for staying balanced and grounded. Giving to others shows what our priorities are. The people we serve through our giving are blessed, and we are also blessed with great feelings for helping others. CEO Kids we've interviewed have also noted that those who give to others often see increases in media coverage as well as increases in revenue as people love to be able to support individuals and businesses who are helping others.

We have been inspired learning about the amazing and charitable acts of CEO Kids, who better their communities in real, meaningful ways. These CEO Kids clearly offer the most pessimistic skeptic something to consider. Let's look at just a few examples of CEO Kids and the charity they provide.

Teen and "tween" sisters Tiffany, Twana, and Victoria Williams were all outgoing, confident individuals with several talents. They wanted their talents to make a difference and were inspired to start "Drive Safe," an organization that provides signs and other materials to help motorists be aware of other drivers with special needs or who are just learning to drive. Sometimes they raise money for their organization by performing, using their singing and dancing talents.

Jenni Smart, of JenniRadio, who as the youngest independent radio host in America (she started at the age of six), toured forty-eight states as a traveling radio host and has been sponsored by Hewlett Packard and others. She feels that the biggest blessing from her business is the charitable work she's been able to do. "I've met a lot of great people. And I have had the chance to help a lot of people too. I've learned a lot about the world, who needs help, and what we can do."

Alex Hodara learned that many of the random things that people wanted to give to charity *couldn't* be given to charity because of its condition, certain rules and regulations, or for other reasons. Alex started selling these non-donatable items on eBay, and donated portions of the profits to charity, such as $3000 to the Children's Specialized Hospital in New Jersey.

The Barta sisters (Lexi, Romi, Marni, and Berni) learned that one of the biggest needs in children's hospitals is movies to watch to help children pass the time during their long hospital stays. As a result, they created Kid Flicks, whose goal is to provide 100 movies to each hospital in the country. Movies are donated to their organization and Kid Flicks passes them on to hospitals. According to their website, "As of November 6, 2010, Kid Flicks has donated 55,400 movies to 554 different hospitals throughout the United States and South Africa." That is a lot of movies!

Similarly, Aneesha Raghunathan created Hope Line Fashions, a clothing-making industry, after visiting India when she was seventeen. She saw the exploitation of workers and created her company so that women there could work for real living wages, which would create greater opportunities in their lives.

Another example of youth entrepreneurship and charity work comes from Lexxi Saal, founder of LexxiLoves.org, an organization that raises funds for foster care and less fortunate families during the holiday seasons.

Then there is Zack Gooding of Guiltless Giving, who found a way to not only help others, but to also make a profit. His organization makes hygiene kits that can be given to the homeless or others in need and are also perfect for emergency situations.

Zack Gonzalez started his entrepreneurship endeavors based on the needs of his younger brother, who was diagnosed with Autism. He has written a book, hosts a radio show, has a line of clothing, and has sponsored numerous fundraising events, all to support those affect by Autism.

Parents can assist their CEO Kids by helping them connect with charities that can best be served by youth entrepreneurs. They can also help them network with friends, neighbors, and professionals, and assisting them to continue to balance their time and energy. For many CEO

Kids, they are taken seriously—and their businesses are taken more seriously—when others recognize the impact they are having upon their communities.

QUESTIONS FOR REFLECTION

1. How do you feel about charitable giving?
2. Do you contribute to charity on a regular basis?
3. Have you taught your kids to contribute to charity?
4. Spend some time researching and choosing a charity to give some of their time and business income to.

PATIENCE

Another characteristic that seems to be evident among CEO Kids is being patient. Patience, at least how CEO Kids present it, is more about staying committed to the path you have set yourself on, and to believe in yourself. Patience comes through successfully putting off things that are less important for things that are more important.

In a landmark study by Stanford University held in the 1960s, four-year-old children were each offered a marshmallow with specific instructions. They could eat the marshmallow right away, or they could wait for a small amount of time and, if they did not eat the marshmallow, they would be rewarded with an extra marshmallow, essentially doubling their investment and pleasure by simply waiting approximately fifteen minutes. Years after the initial marshmallow experiment, the researcher found that the adults (previously children) who had been

> **Patience is a virtue that keeps CEO Kids grounded and committed.**

able to postpone eating the first marshmallow were more successful and happier in life than those who had not developed that patience in childhood.

Many of the CEO Kids and their parents can attest to the importance of patience or delayed gratification. Earlier in this book we learned about knowledge and experience being cumulative, and patience and cumulative learning definitely work together. Patience is being able to recognize that an experience is a step in the right direction, even if it doesn't turn out the way you or your child would like it.

Ryan Bertrand, founder of App Beast, Inc. and former youth entrepreneur, built a webpage when he was fifteen and invested considerable time in designing it. When the iPhone came out, he decided to switch his focus and worked long and hard learning how to create apps for it. Even though he was able to create apps for the iPhone, the sales for those apps were lacking. Fortunately, Ryan remained true to his goals and was patient with the development process. He recognized that his talents with creating apps would make him even better, and went on to create a popular app, "App Bot Pro," which "skyrocketed to number two in the Top Paid list of the Apple AppStore."

Steven Gordon of Tattoo ID says this about the importance of patience in business and how it relates to respect:

> Patience and persistence is crucial because things do not happen overnight. People may not respond to your e-mails for weeks, but you still answer them as if they responded immediately. This brings up another important characteristic: treat everyone with respect. Even though their skill set might not be appealing to you now, they can come in handy down the line.

Andrew Hill's main entrepreneurial efforts began when he was fourteen, after he jokingly told a friend he would take the friend's large fish tank. His friend wanted to get rid of the tank and was glad to give it to him. Having the new fish tank motivated Andrew to learn more about fish and aquariums, and he realized it was very expensive, particularly for an unemployed teen. Andrew feels that patience is a major trait that he had to learn in order to be successful. Through his business, Rumford Aquatics, he grows much of his own products, which takes considerable time. He also has developed patience in working with and talking with others who know little about the business and tease him because they think that the "moss" he's growing is really some kind of drug or something.

Despite a disability, Chris Gross pursued his dreams of web design and going to college, and said,

My advice to CEO Kids is don't be in a hurry. Every day is a learning experience and a chance to grow. I always think I'm behind the curve, but I believe everything is moving in a direction for your success. Slow down. If you're dedicated to the cause, even if it's slow right now, it'll come. Be patient, and eventually the doors open up.

Andrew and Rachel Scott, the parents of Hayleigh Scott, creator of Hayleigh's Cherished Charms, shared the following example of Hayleigh's patience:

When Hayleigh was five, she approached us with some drawings of hearing-aid charms that we had trouble interpreting. A few years later, she drew more pictures and had the vocabulary available to explain to us what she had in mind for charms, tube twists, and scrunchies for hearing aids. Her ideas were great! We then proceeded to help her apply for a provisional patent and eventually a full patent from the U.S. Patent Attorney office.

Receiving the provisional patent and applying for the full patent took a lot longer than we anticipated. Also, no one in the immediate family had any experience with domain names, opening a website, maintaining and updating a website, and utilizing Paypal.

QUESTIONS FOR REFLECTION
1. What things in life have you had to have patience for?
2. How do you implement patience in your own life?
3. How do you teach it to your kids?
4. How does patience keep the young entrepreneur and their parents grounded in things that are most important?

HOW IS YOUR ATTITUDE?

Scan the QR code below or go to page 207 to find out what it says.

_____

RISK TASKING

Taking risks is another strong characteristic for CEO Kids—and all entrepreneurs, for that matter. The key is to balance patience with taking risks in a way that encourages youth entrepreneurs to take risks at the appropriate time as well as to develop skills for rebounding when some risks backfire. Teaching them to take calculated risks and

> "When you run your own business you get a chance to be as creative as you want and if you don't succeed at first, you can continue to try. Some of my ideas have failed, but I know it's okay if I continue to try until I get them right." —Sydney Powell, founder of SS Brandz

to make sure they do their research—weighing the pros and cons of the risk—is important. Some of the risks that may be required include personal change, financial investments, and administrative choices in terms of marketing, growth, and staffing.

As parents, it's sometimes difficult to watch our children take risks because we know there is the potential for failure and pain. Sometimes it's our own fears of being (or being viewed as being) incompetent parents, or perhaps we remember the struggles and hardships we experienced as youth and do not want our own children to experience those same things.

Michael Savage, who started his web design business, Red Metal Box, when he was seventeen, appreciates that his parents let him make and learn from his own mistakes.

> They've given me the space and they've said, well you can make your own mistakes and you learn from your mistakes more than you learn from your successes. So that's definitely what I would encourage. Not that you should make a lot of mistakes. It's just that you definitely do learn from mistakes more than you do successes unfortunately.

Michael's comments reminded us of Domino's Pizza, who took a risk by shamelessly acknowledging that their pizza "tastes like cardboard," then took risks to develop a new pizza that more people liked. Whether it's pizza, web design, or learning to walk, we all can learn a great deal if we simply remember to learn from our mistakes and to take risks even if they backfire every once in awhile.

Fraser Doherty of the U.K. knows about taking risks. When he was a teen, he and a friend asked a neighbor for a box of eggs, hoping each would hatch. Although their parents weren't thrilled with the idea, they placed the eggs near a cable TV box, hoping to keep the eggs warm.

Amazingly a few weeks later, four of the eggs hatched. We raised the chicks in the house and gave them names and when they were grown we put them in the back garden to lay eggs. That was my first-ever little business. Unfortunately, one afternoon, my chicken-farming career was cut short when the local fox decided to eat my chickens for dinner. So that put an end to that."

"If there's one thing that's more important than people skills, it's the ability to learn from failure and to control your own thoughts and focus." Clinton Skakun, web designer

The egg and chicken failure didn't put an end to his willingness to take risks, or to his success. Fraser is the founder of SuperJam, a highly successful natural jam company that received a generous loan from Princess Trust, run by Prince Charles, because of Fraser's youthful entrepreneurial spirit.

One of the biggest "risks" young entrepreneurs must take is self-promotion. Keith J. Davis, Jr., speaker, author, actor, model, and founder of the K. Jerrold Enterprises, Inc., empowers, educates, and motivates young people to become future leaders through thought-provoking seminars, writings, and networking functions. He encourages others to:

> Promote. You've got to be thinking of getting involved in business, especially at a young age. In the beginning, you have to be your biggest promoter. One thing I did, even when I was young, was introduce myself when at events. "I'm Keith J. Davis Jr., young entrepreneur aspiring kind of thing." So you definitely be your biggest promoter. You definitely have to promote because you could have the greatest idea in the world, but if nobody knows about it, it's just another great idea.

Young serial entrepreneur Dale Stephens started a flower-delivery service as a young teen, then sold his photos and blogging services. He shares,

> Know how to talk about yourself. Know how to talk to adults. Be comfortable talking in front of an audience. And basically, in general, build your self-confidence. Be confident and don't ever take no for an answer, even though people question [what you're trying to do].

Dale knows first-hand what he is about, as he is currently developing a new social movement called UnCollege and has done more than his fair share of pitching and presenting around the world.

Savannah Britt, founder of *Girl Pez* magazine, knows a lot about promoting herself and her business.

> Young entrepreneurs should submit press releases constantly, three to four per month. I'm posting links on social media like crazy. Take advantage of press releases. You have to put your name out there. I send my press releases to newspapers, local and bigger outlets. Send it specifically to those who are likely to promote your story—not to those who won't bother with it.

We recommend educating yourself about press releases to avoid some common mistakes. Consider reviewing *The Frugal Book Promoter* by Carolyn Howard-Johnson for some great advice on press releases, personal brand promotion, and selling your products and services.

It's time, if you're not there already, to be comfortable with your child taking risks—and, at times, failing. Parents who let their youth entrepreneurs take risks learn that risk-taking (along with success *and* failure) is inherent in the process of growth.

> "Networking is the key to business, or whatever you do in life. That is exactly why I printed 100 business cards before my trip to the Olympics, and I came back with only 20. All you have to do is meet the person, tell them what you do, then reference your website, etc. to grow your business." —Daniel Wetter, teen journalist and reporter for the 2010 Winter Olympics

Janita Pavelka, mother of four young entrepreneurs, has taught entrepreneurship classes and explains it this way:

It's important for these children to take risks. They're not as fearful and they don't have as much to lose financially. They seem to take loss and risks better than adults—there's not as much fear. As an adult and parent, you need to put your fears aside, they're going to have rejections, or they may not make money—that's okay. If they can get out to interact with people, how to give charity, provide change, or other things, they have so much to gain. You have to allow them to do it.

Johnna Johnson, mother of Ben Johnson, addresses the need for allowing a child to take risks and to allow them to learn from their own experience.

I think the biggest thing is to not be the boss, because as a parent you want to be—but you have to step back and allow them to be. If they're going off in the wrong direction, you can help, but in a gentle manner, and be careful to separate mom from business partner idea. Give them the reins as much as you can. If you see them ready to jump off a cliff, point it out to them and let them see it for themselves and work it out themselves.

Bradley Ericson started in business at thirteen by selling candy at school. To Bradley, selling candy was fun and he didn't worry about whether it was a viable business. Viable business or not, through his experiences selling candy he learned to deal with customers and how to start and grow businesses, which finally led to founding 3-Second Receipts. His work with 3-Second Receipts led to him being named College Entrepreneur of the Year (2009) by *Entrepreneur*

Magazine. Here's what Bradley says about taking risks as a young entrepreneur: "My dad recognized that I was young enough to recover from my mistakes. And I thank him for that mentality."

Kerri Hopkins, mother of Kohl Davis, who fixes and sells Xboxes, reminds us of our responsibility as parents as our kids grow their businesses and take risks. "Be there for them when they're disappointed and focus on the great things they're accomplishing, not the setbacks. Be realistic that setbacks happen; when a door closes, a window opens."

Robert Brooks and Sam Goldstein, in *Raising Resilient Children*, describe children who are resilient to challenges and those who aren't based on the attitude children have toward making mistakes.

"There is a significant difference in the way in which resilient children view mistakes compared with non-resilient children. Resilient children tend to view mistakes as opportunities for learning. In contrast, children who are not very hopeful experience mistakes as an indication that they are failures. In response to this pessimistic view, they are likely to retreat from challenges, feeling inadequate and blaming others for their problems. Thus, if parents are to raise resilient children, they must help them develop a healthy outlook about mistakes from an early age." (p. 13).

Emil Motycka, youth entrepreneur and owner of Motycka Enterprises, LLC., gives his advice about being resilient:

You have to stay in control. Otherwise it shows to everyone you're working with. It's important to stay optimistic—confident but not cocky. It's important to remember that people, whether they are your customers or your workers, are human and everyone makes mistakes.

QUESTIONS FOR REFLECTION:
1. How often do you take risks?
2. In what ways do you encourage your kids to take risks?
3. What is one risk that you have been putting off that you could take today?

6

CEO KID PILLAR #4: OUTCOME

*I*t's more about the journey than the destination. It's cliché, but so true. Whether the goal is to sell lemonade on the corner or to become CEO of a multi-million dollar organization, CEO Kids learn and experience more than they ever imagined when working to reach their goals. We cannot emphasize enough how important it is to keep a small journal or record of your CEO Kid's accomplishments, as they will pay huge dividends in the future. This journal or resume should keep track of the skills, events, accomplishments, and experiences that can be used to help fill out future employment and college applications, media requests, and even when writing a book! Youth often struggle with understanding how one event or skill will benefit them in the future, and that's where parents can be incredibly helpful.

TURNING PASSION INTO PROFIT

We know many kids, as well as adults, who are entrepreneurs who love what they do so much that they would likely do it for free, and that is awesome. However, the truth is that the world we live in does require money to exist, so we want to be sure that we talk about the financial rewards of entrepreneurship and the importance of learning to use money wisely and have it work for you.

"Find your passion and there are always ways to get paid for anything you do."--- Chris Hughes, a juggler and founder of Begin Smart Success.

While some young entrepreneurs have made a relatively small amount of money, others have made millions, so we want you to know that the sky is the limit. Do not put a limit on your earning potential (whether you are an adult or a CEO Kid). While not desiring to contradict ourselves, we want to offer a warning that while millions in income is possible, it cannot be the only measure of success or you are setting yourself and your kids up for possible disappointment.

In the following pages, you will get to meet some of the young entrepreneurs we interviewed who experienced huge financial success for themselves or for the non-profits they founded.

Consider David Wilkinson, founder/owner of OpTank, said of the following about one of his surprises when it came to financial success:

"I've experienced a lot of surprises in my business. For example, PayPal shut down my account $25,000 into my first product launch because the European Union thought that someone who is making that much money that quickly must be money laundering." (Fortunately, the issue was resolved when David provided documentation showing he was running a legitimate successful business).

Then there is Olivia Bennett, fine artist, who was also featured in *Richest Kids of America* by Mark Victor Hansen. "When I was ten, I did my first art show and the first weekend I sold twenty-four paintings and made almost $2,000.00." Olivia was diagnosed with leukemia at a young age, and has overcome it, and now runs her own art gallery and teaches art and painting lessons.

Emil Motycka started his lawn-mowing business in middle school and was making over six figures a year by the time he was out of high school.

Ryan Ross started selling eggs when he was three, and then transitioned into several other businesses including real estate, which has now grown into a nearly million-dollar portfolio, much of which he reinvests into building homes for families in third-world countries.

Juliette Brindak took her love of art and created an online community website as well as a line of books that has grossed millions of dollars in the last few years.

Another financial aspect of business that is appealing for kids and adults, but not so loved by the Internal Revenue Service, is that of bartering. Some of the kids we interviewed got all kinds of things in exchange for their business products or services.

For example, George Drage loved eating Mexican food and bartered his services of web design for food.

> I said to the restaurant, "Why don't you have a website? You're a restaurant, you should have a website." And so I just talked to them. I said, "All right, if we make a deal, I will come here once a week for a certain amount of times, you won't charge me for my food and I'll have a website for you." That's a bargain!

Our children barter all the time, and it has not only allowed them to get things they want without handing over money, it has allowed them to develop powerful negotiation skills. Jacob, our son, barters tech work in exchange for us buying pizza for him. He barters with people he has met via his YouTube channel for things like graphic design, video intros, and tech-related products. Clarissa, our daughter, bartered cake decorating and sewing lessons in exchange for childcare services.

The exchange of money provides great lessons, and the IRS certainly wants an accounting of money being made so they can collect taxes, but there is definitely a place for bartering in the world of young entrepreneurs. Another thing that bartering can open up is the development of business relationships that would not otherwise exist if the hurdle of money had not been overcome.

QUESTIONS FOR REFLECTION

1. Did you grow up in a low-income environment or in affluence?
2. How did your upbringing influence how you view money?
3. Do you think that kids should only be allowed to make a certain amount of money?
4. Do you believe it is possible for your child to be monetarily successful?
5. What are you willing to do to support your child financially in their business journey?
6. What are the top three interests or hobbies of your CEO Kid?
7. Which interest or hobby has the greatest number of options for producing income rather than just costing money?
8. What action could you take to assist your child in creating income from their interest or hobby?

ARE YOU READY FOR A GREAT EXPERIENCE?

Scan the QR code below or go to page 207 to find out what it says.

CONFIDENCE

In addition to money, there are many more "end result" benefits for CEO Kids. These tend to be intangible, or difficult to measure, but nonetheless exist. One of the biggest results for CEO Kids is the incredible confidence they gain.

Dallas Crilley, author of *Kidpreneuer*, said:

> They are paying me to speak. It makes me feel a lot cooler than I really am. So let me get this straight, you are flying me out, paying for my expenses, and paying me to speak so that you can listen to me and laugh at my jokes. I feel like I should be paying them. So cool!

Lori Costigan, mother of youth entrepreneur and professional speaker Michael Costigan says,

> Make sure your children believe in themselves. Let them know they can do whatever they want to do. That's something I've always believed. Some people don't believe that—or they think they're stuck with whatever their family has or is like.

Jaqui Haggerty, mother of Steven Haggerty of Salut World, sums things up pretty well when she says,

Believe in your child. Do not put them down, even if your experience tells you that maybe what they are saying and trying to do may be difficult. Let them try to find out for themselves. Never tell them they cannot do something. Put forward a couple of alternative suggestions and let them think about it and come to their own conclusions. Times change. As parents, we do not live in their world, we are not part of their generation, therefore they understand a lot more about what their world needs than we do. Be non-judgmental and totally supportive. Be there and be prepared to do some problem solving and put together some pieces every now and then...even in the middle of the night!

Kim Hix, mother of fifteen-year-old Zack, founder of Good Boy Roy T-shirt Designs and Animations, agrees. "I am not one to analyze what has already been done, you can't go back and re-do the past. I am a big dreamer and believer, so I just go with my gut. This was a very impulsive 'just do it' idea." Several youth entrepreneurs and their parents echoed this *"Just do it"* philosophy.

QUESTIONS FOR REFLECTION
1. How is your child's confidence?
2. What are three ways that you can begin to increase their confidence and encourage their success in business?

FAMILY COHESION

In our completely biased opinion, the best part of being a CEO Kid is the enthusiasm and solidarity it provides within the family. This is because families learn to unite by supporting the business of each of their kids.

Zhu Shen, mother of Perry Chen of Perry's Previews, offers her experience about the bonding that takes place.

> If you pay attention to your kids, you will learn about what they enjoy. You will learn what will motivate them based on what they are interested in. That way you can grow with your kids. For me, it's a deep bonding experience in working with him on the movie reviews. I learn about his heart and soul, what he's thinking about—it's almost a spiritual experience for me. We've been on an incredible journey, and I am amazed at Perry's accomplishments.

Zhu also mentioned that it was a learning experience for her. She grew in knowledge and awareness, along with her son.

Mary Sarah Gross, a musician and singer, says this about her family and how they work together to support her in business:

> "The family helps out a lot. I think that brings us closer together—we are closer knit." —Ben Johnson, age sixteen, founder of Running Wild Paintball

> My sister and I love writing together. Me and my sister—actually my whole family—we just all kind of pitch in and write. My brother [Chris Gross, also in this book] helps a lot with the website. My mom helps me with everything. She helps me if we go to photo shoots, and just everything like that. My dad, he's more on the music side, so he helps me a lot on the guitar and he's in some of my videos if you go on YouTube. He also has a lot of connections. My whole family pretty much supports me. They all support me 100% and I'm so thankful to have a family.

Travis Woodward of Dinosoar Studios, a successful video production company, said,

> I do almost everything by myself, except my mom and step-dad review my final products to make sure they are as professional as possible. I'm learning how to do invoicing and bookkeeping right now, and my mom is helping me with that.

Suzanna Duly, fifteen, founder of North Shore T-shirts, said, "My dad loves it, he loves helping me. He thinks it's so cool, and we've bonded because of it."

Many youth entrepreneurs and their families gain this enthusiasm and loyalty to the business because they made a choice to be strong as a family. It sounds easy, but being truly committed to a cause, purpose, or vision as a family takes work and the outcome can be significant. According to

John C. Maxwell[8] "No team has ever achieved extraordinary results without a 100 percent commitment to the cause and a common vision. . . To have full commitment, a team must understand the vision, contribute to it, own it, and, eventually, pass it up."

The fact that you are reading this book attests to the reality that you are interested in that common vision and a great relationship with your young entrepreneur (or soon-to-be CEO Kid).

We recommend having frequent conversations as a family to determine what each person's role is, where their interest is, and how each member can support the other. These conversations may feel awkward at first, but it will give your youth entrepreneur (and you) the skills of meaningful communication and dealing with challenges. Go into these conversations with the recognition that the family (including each member's goals and dreams) is more important than the business itself; the business is just a mechanism for accomplishing those dreams. Look back on the reasons for why the business was first created, and ask if the goals are still the same. If not, then what are the new goals? Do not become so wed to the business that you feel compelled to force your youth entrepreneur to give more time and energy than they are willing to give. Remember your role in the family and realize that role may not always carry over into determining the direction of your youth entrepreneur's business.

Jeff Gross, father of Hunter Gross, fifteen, of ProjectKool, a company with the purpose of combating global warming, agrees that a successful business will do much more than just improve the business. He says,

---

[8] "Succeeding Together: The Core Values of a Winning Team" in SUCCESS, February, 2011, pages 16-17

A successful business takes life to another level, a better level, and it helps everybody communicate, be creative, it's an open forum, people are just kind of tossing ideas and bouncing ideas off of each other, and I think we all know that the more we talk and the more we communicate, chances are the better things will be.

QUESTIONS FOR REFLECTION

1. What does family support and cohesion look like to you?
2. How are the members of your family already supporting each other in life and business?
3. What are some ways that you can connect more as a family?
4. What is the best time of day or week to connect with your family and to begin to support one another more in life and in business?

CREATIVITY

One of the biggest surprises for many youth entrepreneurs is that their business serves as an outlet and developer of their creativity. Creativity is also a component necessary to launch the business and make it grow. The business can not exist without some amount of creativity. Being able to expand upon one's creativity is what makes the business fun, exciting, and "new" all over again. Having creativity allows an entrepreneur to explore new products and services and find ways to improve functions and processes. Creative problem-solving allows business owners to tackle the sometimes daunting challenges that come from starting and growing a business.

Emily and Robin Johnson, parents of Erin, Lachlan, and Jake Johnson, the founders of Flipoutz, explained, "It was never really about making money or even business in the beginning. We tried to foster creativity in the children and thinking outside the box, and let their interests and ideas lead us."

When Stephen Ou, a young app developer, programmer, and designer, was asked what he thinks are the most important skills he has that have helped him in business, he provided the following answer:

I honestly can't judge which one is the most important. It's a combination of many things. Determination is needed to keep trying when bad moments come, especially at the beginning. Creativity is needed to come up with things that set myself and my software apart. Responsibility is needed to recognize mistakes, share lessons after messing up, especially when my products are consumer driven. Nothing would work without the combination of them.

Zack Hix of Good Boy Roy clothing said something very similar in response to the same question, "You definitely need creativity and a good imagination."

Kristyn Heath, nineteen, who started Passive Devices, a technology and music business of making prototypes of gadgets such as earphones, thoroughly enjoyed how her business accepted and increased her creative spirit. "I love the freedom in doing what you want to do, to make your own schedule, to choose what you want, and there is a lot of creativity and opportunities for owning a business at a young age."

QUESTIONS FOR REFLECTION
1. In what ways can you foster creativity in your child?
2. Who are some of your mentors for creativity and how can you follow their example?
3. When do you and your child get the best creative ideas, and how can you set aside more time in your day to let the creativity flow?

7

OVERCOMING LIMITATIONS

While we do not want to limit anyone's enthusiasm for youth entrepreneurship, it's important to be honest with ourselves that there may be some challenges along the way. Many of the youth entrepreneurs and their parents told us, "If I only knew then what I know now." This doesn't mean that they wouldn't still pursue entrepreneurism, but rather that they were setback by challenges because they initially did not know how to overcome them. Fortunately, this chapter specifies not only the difficulties with youth entrepreneurship, but it also helps you overcome those challenges

FINANCES

Financial hardship is one of the most common limitations that wannabe youth entrepreneurs and their families experience. Businesses, whether run by adults or youth, often require some level of start-up money. For some families this financial capital is easier to obtain than it is for others.

But not investing financially in a business, particularly your child's business, is primarily due to fear. Sometimes that fear can serve as a motivator, and at other times it can paralyze. Let's take a look at some of those fears.

In an uncertain economy, it can be a scary thing to place money in a venture when you are nervous about the viability of that business. It's particularly painful to give up money when the money was initially prioritized for something else, like bills. These kinds of fears frequently steer parents into what we like to call the "No Camp." They focus more on what can't happen. No, you can't start a business because we don't have the money. No, I don't have any money to give you. No, what if it's destined to fail?

Focusing on the lack of funds leads to fear, and can discourage your child from following his or her vision, now and in the future. If you don't have enough money, or even if you don't have *any* money, there still is a way to financially support your child with their dreams of entrepreneurship.

Several CEO Kids developed their own business simply because their parents told them to go earn their *own* money (rather than the parents giving money to them for their wants or to build their business). Parents were tired of pretending (and flatly refused) to be their child's ATM machine or responsible for each and every financial decision their child made. Nothing is wrong with financially investing in your child's business, but it's equally or perhaps more powerful to tell them to financially invest in it themselves. It's okay to let your child brainstorm, do the legwork, and even fail—as long as you help them see that it's part of the process for achieving. Children are creative, and *very* creative when given the chance, so don't be surprised (or shocked or discipline them) when your youth entrepreneur tells you he got the money for the business by simply asking customers entering and exiting a grocery store for the money. If you are concerned about how far your child will go to get the money, then you better be part of the process.

Rydel Hemmings, fourteen, founder of Rydels Adventure and youth author, became interested in business because her mom, Barbie Lee Hemmings, told her she had to earn the money herself if she and her sister wanted to buy something. Barbie Lee told us,

> When my daughters had really expensive tastes as young children, I told them if they wanted to buy what they wanted they had to come up with it. So they really had no choice but to become entrepreneurs! They started thinking about business because they saw a really cool thing for $400 and wanted to buy it. I asked them if they had the money for it. They didn't, so they had to start thinking about how to make money.

When you are able to turn the conversation of "No you can't have that" into "How can you create that?" you release yourself from the conversation of lack and turn it into a conversation of possibility. So many kids and adults are focused on what we *can't* have instead of what we *do* have—and what we can do to create what we want. Teaching kids at a young age that they have the power to work for, and to create for themselves, the things they want is such a huge gift.

Another financial challenge for some youth entrepreneurs is money management and watching out for the bottom line. Mrs. Errico, mother of Lorenzo Errico, former youth entrepreneur and founder of Formation Skateboard Company, said the following:

> One of the main challenges was to keep him focused on the cost and profit ratio. As a young entrepreneur it is easy to lose your focus. It is especially hard with his line of business—skateboards and skateboarding products—as all his friends wanted discounts and free gifts.

Mrs. Errico has a great point that we have experienced personally with our own children and that other parents have expressed as well. Your child is a real business person, but because of their age others may try to take advantage of them. Having an open dialogue with them about what they can actually charge on the open market is important. Sometimes you may even need to step in and stand up for them when you see they are not being respected for the value they are giving in products or services.

The younger, the better, if parents are going to teach their children the importance of financial accountability. Quinn van der Gulik was three years old when he wanted to run a lemonade stand. His mom and aunt helped, but his mom said that the start-up capital had to be paid back.

> My mommy told me the cups and the lemonade were a "Business Loan" that I had to pay back first before I could take any of the money I made. I didn't mind because otherwise I wouldn't have had any lemonade to sell. So that was okay.

Parents can help by reassuring their youth entrepreneur that their service or product is worth being paid for, and to encourage them to keep a balance sheet. Dreams are powerful and positive, but without a plan of assessment they can become dangerously expensive.

QUESTIONS FOR REFLECTION

1. What are some things that you can do to financially support your CEO Kid and their new business without just giving them the money outright?
2. What are some things that your CEO Kid can do to earn the money on their own to start their business?
3. Are there things in your home that you are no longer using that you or your CEO Kid could sell to come up with the money to start their business?

AGE

Age can work for, or it can work against, your youth entrepreneur. Many of the negative aspects of being young are compensated for by having supportive parents, who help where help is needed. The biggest factor regarding age, however, is how others perceive your youth entrepreneur, and how that impacts their clientele.

> **In a popular Disney show, Phineas and Ferb, the main characters are asked, "Aren't you boys a little young to build your own roller coaster?" Phineas and Ferb look at the adult asking the question and answer, "Yes, we are." And then they build it.**

"Both my sons have achieved by their own resources and have built successful business out of nothing. Age is also challenging, as some people do not take young business people seriously. Both my sons have had to work twice as hard to prove themselves as being professional, reliable, mature business people. They have proved themselves and receive great feedback and respect from their clients."— Jacqui Haggerty, mother of Steven Haggerty

For some, being young is a huge advantage! Some people have a harder time telling young children "no", which leads to an increase in sales for young entrepreneurs. Imagine two visits to your home, one by a child and another by an adult, each who tries to sell you a candy bar to earn money for a bike they want to buy. We know which one you're more likely to buy from – the child!

We, as a society, are more likely to have a "soft spot" for children than we are to have for adults. That's because of the different expectations we have for each. The expectations that society has for children will often help your child gain access to promoting their business. You'll hear words like, "Wow—she has a business and she is only nine years old!" Or, "He's fixing computers—isn't he only twelve?" Your child may earn admiration, which will fuel free publicity, increased sales, and more.

On the other hand, several CEO Kids find that others feel that their young age is a disqualifier for a "real business." The "cute factor" for a child only goes so far—some people don't believe children when they say they are part of a serious business endeavor. They are okay with the idea while it's a dream, hobby, or fad, but when it's a true business it's a different story.

Occasionally people can take advantage of a youth entrepreneur's vision by making them sell a product or service for less than they should—simply because they don't think a child "should" be able to make real money. Parents definitely need to step up to the plate on this; how parents talk about their child's business will make a huge difference in how others respond to your youth entrepreneur. And how your CEO Kid presents his or her self will largely determine how others look at whether or not the business is legitimate.

Hannah Braboy, owner of Hannah Braboy Photography, was eleven when she started her business. She said, "My age honestly doesn't affect things much at all because I conduct myself in an adult-like manner and prove to others that they can trust me."

Similarly, Donny Ouyang, founder of Kinkarso, a technology company that helps others develop websites, recommends being as good at providing the same service as those who are older than you so that age is never an issue for customers. By overcompensating on delivery of the goods or services promised, your CEO Kid will more often than not be able to overcome any perceived negative effects tied to their age.

We also really liked Brandi Thomas' advice. Brandi, founder and instructor of Ballroom by Brandi, says,

As a sixteen year old, I had clients walk in for their first ballroom dance lesson with a look of shock on their face. They saw a young girl and wondered what they had gotten themselves into. Even now at nineteen years old, every time I meet with a new client, I have to prove that I am worth both their time and their money. The easiest way to accomplish this is to act like an adult business owner. Have confidence: give your clients a firm handshake, stand up straight, look them in the eye, don't use phrases such as "um", "like", or "you know". Good communication is key. If you act like an adult business owner, your clients will give you their respect and their patronage.

Jacob Cass of Just Creative Design also has some strong insight for young entrepreneurs.

I use my age as a promotional tool kind of thing because people are quite surprised when they realize my age. I kind of use it to my advantage. When I promote myself, I just say what you can achieve if you really put your mind to it and age is no matter. I know many popular bloggers at the moment who are about sixteen years old and they're making quite a lot of money just by writing online and it's just really amazing. Age just doesn't mean a thing at all.

For many youth entrepreneurs, their age is both an asset and a liability. Thirteen-year-old Adora Svitak is a speaker, author, and teacher. She was seven when she published *Flying Fingers.*

> I try to make age irrelevant to business success, because everyone ages every year, and good CEOs know that a measure of quality is longevity. In that vein, I don't like being referred to as a prodigy. That said, I do try to use my age to relate to peer groups, to speak for causes I believe in, and provide points of view that are rarely heard (for instance, speaking about youth empowerment to adults at conferences). My age may sometimes be a "wow factor," but I don't aggressively market it as such. Being thirteen has helped me connect with the school-age audience, but at the same time it's exposed me to restrictions from adults toward youth. Ultimately, I think that getting started early has allowed me to have practice that many other kids haven't had.

Nick Tart, founder of JuniorBiz and 14 Clicks, started business very young and is currently in college. He believes that starting at a young age is often an advantage simply because others think youth lack knowledge, and a lot of people want to give them free advice.

> The fact that people were willing to give me free advice definitely helped me out in the long run. I really appreciate it. I learned something from almost every conversation I had with people. If I were older they'd be billing me for their time and advice.

Earlier we wrote about donating proceeds to charity. This serves as a powerful reflection of how mature the child is, and how others will look at your child and their business. Some CEO Kids mentioned use of freebies, samples, and trials on their products and services to "prove" to the potential clients that what they were offering was valuable and warranted the price tag attached to the product or service.

QUESTIONS FOR REFLECTION
1. How do you view your child's age in relationship to them wanting to start a business?
2. What are the pros for them regarding their age and their business endeavor?
3. What are some things they can work on or that they will need to overcome where age is concerned?

FEAR AND DOUBT

As mentioned, fear and doubt can jeopardize youth entrepreneurship—if you let them. The truth is that every—or nearly every—CEO Kid faces fears and doubts. "Will others want to buy my product?" "What can I say to people?" "Will they'll laugh at me?"

Young adult and former CEO Kid Mandee Widrick, owner of ChargedUp Media and founder of Horse Family magazine, said she was afraid of talking with new people and doing things she didn't completely understand at the time. But going through it gave her confidence in herself.

The real concern, however, is what to do to confront those fears and doubts. Some of the most common fears have to do with public speaking, making the sale, and fear of failing. How one addresses these concerns will set the stage for failure or success.

Public speaking is a very common fear, but it can be particularly frightening if one's self-esteem is tied to whether people like your youth entrepreneur's idea or not. We recommend checking out books, videos, and audios on public speaking to help your young entrepreneur gain practice and knowledge about public speaking. It is also suggested that your CEO Kid practice giving their "elevator speech" in front of the mirror and on camera; this will help them see how they appear to others and what they need to work on. An elevator speech is a brief (15–60 seconds) script that tells others who you are, what you do, how you can help them, and possibly what you're looking for in an ideal client. Your CEO Kid should use every opportunity to introduce his or her self using their unique elevator speech.

Making the sale only occurs after the elevator speech is given, features and benefits about the product or service have been shared, and concerns of the person that is being presented to have been addressed. How others respond often involves resolving their concerns. Selling will require confidence in oneself and in one's product or services, as well as being knowledgeable about that product and how it compares with similar products or services. Furthermore, successfully selling involves the ability to listen and to match the needs of the client with the benefits of the product or service as well as overcome any objections.

Juliette Brindak, creator of Miss O & Friends, a multi-million dollar company directed toward tween and teen girls, knows about making the sale.

> One of our very first books is a book called, Write On. We were doing a series of little novels, like chapter books, and we thought it would be a really good idea if girls could have a book with their own written stories and poems and have it published. Our publisher said, "No, no, no, no. That's a really bad idea, girls aren't going to read that." We said, "Okay, thank you for that advice but let's ask the girls." We did a poll and we had over 2,000 responses within a few days. And 82% of the girls said they would read a book written by girls themselves over another author. So we took that back to our publishers and said, "I'm sorry, but you're wrong." And they published the book.

One of the things we can do as parents to hedge the fear and doubt is to make sure that our kids feel and know that they are loved. It is much easier to risk and do something you fear when you know you are loved and supported on the home front.

As you take time to praise your children and let them know they are loved, you will notice some wonderful benefits. Some of the things we have found in our own children are that when they feel loved, heard, valued, and validated the failures, obstacles, setbacks, and haters will be much easier to take. Empowering children to be able to embrace fear and overcome doubt with courageous action is priceless.

QUESTIONS FOR REFLECTION

1. What are three things you can do today to show your child that you love and support them?
2. What are some things that you have been fearing, and what are the actions steps you can take to "face your fear and do it anyway"?
3. What fears do your children have? What are some action steps that your kids can take to face their fears?

LACK OF TIME

Time is perhaps the scarcest commodity among families today. School, homework, sports, other extracurricular activities, and, yes, Facebook all vie for our hours. Perhaps you and your child want to develop youth entrepreneurship, and you really do not have any spare moments to fit it in. That's okay—it simply may not be the right time to develop that business.

Most of us, however, have more time than we think. Much of a person's free time, and especially of an adolescent, is consumed by watching television, texting, browsing the internet, or on social networking sites. We encourage you and your child to keep a diary or to record the time when you are using media for non-school or non-employment reasons, and see what it tallies up to. We think you just might be surprised!

We don't want to give the impression that having fun is wrong, or that relaxing is to be discouraged. The point is that, for most of us, we can make fostering our child's entrepreneurship activities a priority, and we can encourage our kids to make room in the schedule to grow their business and empower their future, even if it's just fifteen to thirty minutes a day.

QUESTIONS FOR REFLECTION

1. Is there time before, during, or after school or on the weekend that your child could begin to grow a business online or in person?
2. Could an activity that your child is doing be substituted instead for engagement in entrepreneurship?
3. Are there things in your schedule that you really could let go of or say "no" to in order to make time to support your child in a business?

BURN OUT

Getting burned out or losing one's drive and commitment in one's business is always possible. Fortunately, following the steps and principles in this book will reduce the frequency and severity or even the occurrence at all. Maintaining vision, proper action, and engaging in skills and practices that foster a positive attitude are all needed to stick with, to enjoy, and to be successful with business. If you are at the stage of burn out, or your child is, it may be a good idea to review the chapters that focus on vision, action, and attitude. Some of the ideas from those chapters were designed to help you and your youth entrepreneur maintain balance so that you can enjoy the work.

Your youth entrepreneur may also get burned out if they feel significant pressure in their business, social life, or schooling. The line is sometimes blurry between being supportive and stressing your child, and it's even more important that you evaluate whether you've crossed that line. If you have, be forthright with your child and ask for their forgiveness and for their input as to how *they* think you can be more supportive. Allow for open communication in your family so that children are able and encouraged to tell you when they are feeling pushed, pressured, and forced. When they know that you will listen—and hear them and respect them—they will be willing to share their feelings. Sometimes just allowing them to express what is inside will be enough.

Our daughter had several media opportunities come at her all at once, and because she is a private and reserved person, she was feeling a lot of pressure to perform. She was reaching a breaking point and yelled at us to quit pushing her. When we let her know that she didn't have to do the cooking show, appear on TV, or go to the speaking engagement she was relieved. We let her know that she was capable, and that we knew she could do it and that she would do a great job, but it was her decision as to what to do and what not to do. In the end she decided to do some things and not the others. Giving her control kept her from burning out and quitting her business all together.

QUESTIONS FOR REFLECTION

1. Are you or your kids facing "burn out"?
2. If so, what are some ways that you feel would empower you to regain joy and excitement in life and in business?

FRIENDS

Another factor that comes in to play for youth entrepreneurs is that their friends may sometimes be jealous or worried that a business may in some way jeopardize their network of friends. It's true that running a business can reduce time spent with friends, and it can change the CEO Kid in a way that alters the status quo in that clique. Some adolescents can be cruel to those who wish to go against what is normal among their peers.

Earlier we wrote about the importance of balancing business with the life of a child. It's important to their social and emotional wellbeing to invest their time and energy in their friendships. Friendships also give youth entrepreneurs the ability to de-stress from some of the pressures that a business will provide. The key is balance.

One possibility is to include the CEO Kid's friends in the business endeavor. Pretty much everyone likes to make money, and it can provide status and solidarity within that friendship. Unfortunately, having a friend working with or under you can also be dangerous; friends start out with equal power, but in a business relationship that power shifts to the CEO Kid. We strongly suggest you consider the risks and benefits before having a friend included in the business, or offer a trial period.

Encouraging your kids to make time for friends and to make "being a kid" a priority will help them. Lizzie Marie Likness, owner of Lizzie Marie Cuisine, says,

A lot of people think that if you're a young business owner that you don't have time to do anything fun. For me, Lizzie Marie Cuisine is a lot of fun, but I do enjoy just being a kid sometimes. I have lots of friends who keep me grounded. I still have time to have sleepovers and hang out with friends and all the fun things that are a part of being a teen. Even though Lizzie Marie Cuisine is a big part of my life, it's important to me and my family that I still have the experience of just being a kid and enjoying life.

Another point to consider is setting up some boundaries and guidelines for what things must be done before hanging out with friends. It's important if you want to instill in your kids the need to be responsible in business. Dylan Brooks, founder of Skate Punkz clothing line, says, "I have to do my homework, then I can work with my mom. We discuss where we are and what still needs to be done. Then I can play with my friends."

QUESTIONS FOR REFLECTION
1. In what ways can you facilitate the balance between your child being in business and having fun with friends?
2. Are there boundaries that need to be put in place so that your child doesn't get taken advantage of financially by friends?
3. What are the guidelines you have in place for getting schoolwork done, taking care of business matters, and being with friends or other extracurricular activities?

8

HOW TO GET STARTED

Every child, family, business, and community has
different strengths and needs. Unfortunately, this
means that there is no standard cookie-cutter
approach for youth entrepreneurship. However, there are
guidelines to follow, as given throughout this book. We have
also compiled a list of resources to help you and your child.
Our favorite recommendation is to learn from other youth
entrepreneurs and their families, particularly from those
whose interests, values, or business are similar to your CEO
Kid's.

The answer to the question, "How do we start?" really
encompasses "When do we start?" and "What do we start
with?" The process will take time, but it's okay, too, if
everything does happen at once. Becoming an overnight
success is more of an exception than a rule; for most it will
take time, energy, and patience to reach the desired success.
Emily-Anne Rigal, founder of Schmiddlebopper and creator
of WeStopHate.org, says,

> I think in getting started, the biggest obstacle to overcome is simply just starting. It can be incredibly overwhelming, and whenever I feel as if it's too much, I say to myself, "It's just the beginning, everything that I want to happen will happen, but it isn't all going to happen right this second. One thing at a time." Remembering that it's okay to start small is very important when starting a business.

TAKING RESPONSIBILITY

We started to teach the concept of work when our own children were very small, in fact way before they even thought of owning their own businesses. I (Sarah) have worked from home for over seventeen years and discovered that one of the ways to keep our three kids happy and busy while I worked was to have the children work alongside me throughout the day. Working with me taught them valuable skills over the years, many of which they used to create their own product-based and service-based businesses. When they got older (around 7 years old), I officially put them on payroll and began giving them regular paychecks each month. This not only saved us money in business taxes but it also gave the children consistent income that they could use to learn money-management skills such as saving, budgeting, wise spending, investing, and giving to charity. Once they were on payroll, we began to have them pay for things such as school lunch, clothing, and part of their extra-curricular activities, such as soccer and piano lessons.

Below is a list of activities that I have delegated to my children as well as some that other parent entrepreneurs have hired their young children to do. As children master these activities or other business activities, they will gain confidence and will begin to see what activities they enjoy most. They can then turn those skills into a product or service-based business that is their very own. Having your child do things for you in your business will not only give your child new skills, it will also teach them responsibility and various aspects of life in business. It will open up opportunities to talk to your child about why you are doing what you are doing in business as well as other windows of opportunity for teachable moments. While reading through this list, keep your child in mind and think about the activities that they might enjoy doing that would allow them to develop a business by mastering the skills associated with the business tasks.

- ✓ Sort receipts
- ✓ Enter receipts into the computer accounting program
- ✓ Download statements into Quicken or MS Money
- ✓ Get customer-service campaigns ready: birthday and anniversary cards
- ✓ Send pre-written e-mails
- ✓ Inventory product and samples
- ✓ Rotate and restock product
- ✓ Label products
- ✓ Create new client-information packets
- ✓ Be in charge of recycling within the business
- ✓ Look up addresses and MapQuesting appointments, if you do not have a GPS
- ✓ Make desserts and snacks for appointments
- ✓ Be a hostess/greeter for client-appreciation events
- ✓ Enter product returns
- ✓ Enter clients into databases
- ✓ Research for articles, webinars, presentations
- ✓ Role play with you
- ✓ Pass out business cards to teachers, friends' parents, neighbors, sports coaches, and more
- ✓ Edit video
- ✓ Edit audio
- ✓ Upload files to your web-hosting account
- ✓ Set up for a customer event
- ✓ Pass out flyers in the neighborhood or a parking lot
- ✓ Send card campaigns through Send Out Cards
- ✓ Shred sensitive documents

- ✓ Recycle
- ✓ Social bookmarking
- ✓ Test product
- ✓ Test website links and pages
- ✓ Set up social media
- ✓ Maintain social media
- ✓ Schedule Tweets/Facebook posts/LinkedIn and other such social media updates
- ✓ Transcribe training
- ✓ Approve comments on blogs
- ✓ Download, install, and activate plug-ins on blogs
- ✓ Create graphic design
- ✓ Design web page
- ✓ Set up Squidoo lenses
- ✓ Add products to eBay and take care of the sale of items
- ✓ Give seller and buyer feedback on eBay
- ✓ Read books and take notes on them for you
- ✓ Detail your car, if you have a work vehicle
- ✓ Take messages
- ✓ Dust/clean your work area
- ✓ File papers
- ✓ Burn CDs, DVDs, or other media for your business
- ✓ Make customer-service calls
- ✓ Manage your Google calendar and/or enter dates into http://tungle.me
- ✓ Set up playlists in iTunes
- ✓ Download training CDs to iTunes library and sync things so you are ready to go for your daily education
- ✓ Wrap gifts for clients and prospective clients
- ✓ Make goal posters and other visuals to keep you on track
- ✓ Hold you to the goals you have set, if you know what I mean! (Pay them to "nag" you!)
- ✓ Remove computer viruses
- ✓ Maintain computer disk optimization and defragmentation
- ✓ Install and remove computer programs
- ✓ Maintain computer network
- ✓ Back up data

- ✓ Shop and compare new technology
- ✓ Watch/entertain younger brothers or sisters so you can get your work done
- ✓ Clean the house when you have appointments coming
- ✓ Research domains
- ✓ Purchase domains
- ✓ Add domains to your web hosting
- ✓ Install WordPress or another blogging platform
- ✓ Pack your car for appointments
- ✓ Pack your bags for travel engagements
- ✓ Research the best deals in flights, hotels, and rental cars
- ✓ Research entertainment activities to do alongside business travel appointments
- ✓ Mow and/or weed yard when you are having events in your home
- ✓ Edit photos
- ✓ Design flyers, brochures, cards
- ✓ Convert files to and from PDF
- ✓ Create videos for events
- ✓ Create slide presentations or PowerPoint presentations
- ✓ Organize your office
- ✓ Get rid of old documents in your filing system
- ✓ Design the Christmas card or write the Christmas letter
- ✓ Shine shoes
- ✓ Sew buttons on an outfit
- ✓ Convert traditional pictures to digital format
- ✓ Scrapbook or document business history
- ✓ Set up affiliate accounts
- ✓ Track affiliate campaigns
- ✓ Shrink affiliate and other urls using http://bit.ly
- ✓ Edit documents or E-books
- ✓ Research PLR (Private Label Right) products
- ✓ Maintain password and user name files for all the things that run your business
- ✓ Print expense and income reports
- ✓ Fill product orders
- ✓ Text message clients with a specific text promotion
- ✓ Enter client information and set up phone groups in

    http://phonevite.com
✓   Send messages on Facebook
✓   Create groups on Facebook

When they are old enough to drive, you can add the following:
✓   Make bank deposits
✓   Fill the car with gas
✓   Mail items and get postage
✓   Pick up dry cleaning
✓   Shop for supplies for events or office
✓   Deliver product orders to clients
✓   Pick up mail from the Post Office box...and MORE!

    Ask yourself what things you could start having your children do so that you can begin teaching them business skills and financial literacy, while freeing yourself of tasks that you don't need to be doing in your business.

    Once you have made a list of jobs your kids could help you with, sit down with each of your children and explain that you want to pay them to work for you. Explain any of the tasks that need clarification and ask them which items they would like to start with. Something that has worked really well for me was to take each task and make a video or written instruction of how to do that task so that they could repeat it without me having to show them each time. As you and your children become more proficient at the delegating process, you can walk them through it and ask them to make detailed instructions or videos of each task so that someone else could do it if you or your child were not available to do it or decided you wanted someone else to do it.

    It will be exciting to see which tasks bring the most joy to your kids. Take note of those things and be open to opportunities to start the conversation of ways that they can turn those gifts and talents they are creating into a business.

    The interesting thing is, you don't have to stop with just things you do in your business. Household and life tasks can just as easily be delegated to your kids and provide valuable life, business, and personal development for them.

For example about two years ago, I was feeling overwhelmed as a wife, mom of three, business owner, coach, and youth ministry leader. There just weren't enough hours in the day. We had a family council discussion about helping and being a team. One of the outcomes was that the children could start doing more tasks that took so much of my time and my husband's time. They started doing their own laundry (or at least one load 2x a week), cleaning the kitchen (sweeping, cleaning surfaces, and putting away the dishes 2x a week), as well as making dinner (2x a week). It hasn't been perfect, to be sure, but we set the expectation. The children know that if they want certain privileges at home they get their tasks done.

There have been several great results that have come from this:

1. All three kids have some level of skill now in doing laundry. (No pink clothes, but pairs of pantyhose have been shredded by Velcro - who needs hosiery, right?)
2. We eat dinner nearly every night by 5 P.M. Sometimes the schedule doesn't allow it, but we strive to guard our "dinner time" as family time.
3. My daughter excelled so much in cooking that she wrote her own cookbook and cooks every day! In fact, we all prefer her cooking over everyone else in the house.

Here are just a few of the business skills that were learned:

1. **Task Management:** If we are eating at 5 P.M., they can't start cooking at 4:55 and expect us to have a great meal. They need to think ahead of time about what ingredients we have (no, I am not running them to the store to shop when it is their day to cook!), what they can make with those ingredients, and schedule time for prepping, cooking, and plating.
2. **Customer Service:** If they do a task poorly and the customers (all the other people in the family) complain, they will have to make it right, whether that means doing the task over, buying mom new hose,

cleaning the burned pan of rice, or writing a letter of apology when feelings have been hurt.

3. **Leadership and communication:** Sometimes the kids have come up with other ideas for ways of doing things and it has taken communication skills to get their ideas across to the other members of the family—as well as leadership skills to get the ideas implemented.

I could go on and on but, hopefully, you see that doing chores and making dinner can help you and your kids become more confident in life and even in business.

QUESTIONS FOR REFLECTION

1. What are some things you can start having your children do in your home or office that will help them learn business skills?
2. Are there things you are paying other people to do for you that you could be having your children do?
3. In what areas of your child's life do you see that taking responsibility will have a positive impact?

STEPS FOR GETTING STARTED

If your kids already have ideas and they already know what they are good at, then by all means, help them get started! It's a good idea to plan as much as you can, but planning can only go so far. The key is to begin. Don't worry about everything being perfect.

Here are Seven Steps for helping your child get started in business and create success:

Step 1: Decide On The Business Idea. Help your child to brainstorm ideas for a business and the products and or services that will be offered in the potential businesses. When your son or daughter has narrowed down the ideas to no more than five that they really like, encourage them to contact other people who have a business similar to the one they are hoping to start. Have your child ask the business owner questions about how much it costs to start that business as well as costs to maintain it, where and how to find clients, what is the best business entity structure for the business, how to price the products or services, and anything they would have done differently when they started. Once the business ideas have been researched by interviewing other people in business, help your child decide on the one that will be best to begin right away.

Step 2: Choose The Business Name. Creating a business name can be really fun and it also requires a fair amount of research. Some elements that make a business name great are that it is easy to remember, it describes the business, and it creates an emotion in the potential client. Not every business name has these elements, but they are good points to consider. Do an Internet search to see if the business name being considered is already being used by another established company. Do a at least a basic trademark search http://www.uspto.gov/trademarks/ to see if someone has already trademarked the potential business name. Doing a trademark search on your own is not as thorough as having a lawyer do it for you but it does give you a good idea of what to stay away from when choosing a name. Once you have brainstormed lots of names and have done your research to see that no one else is using the name, it is time pick the name you will use for your business and move on to the next step.

Step 3: Set Up The Business Structure. There are diverse ways to set up a business and the entity chosen depends on personal and business liability and the pros and cons of how the tax law will affect the business owner personally. As a business grows, it can be restructured from one entity to another. The basic choices for entities are: sole proprietorship, partnership, limited partnership, corporation, limited liability company, and cooperatives. Sometimes nothing official needs to be done before a small business gets started. When our son, Jacob, first started selling online, we called the county business office and were told that because he was so young and would likely not be making very much money, he didn't need a license or any official business structure. It is best that you talk to your local government offices and even a lawyer to find out what things need to be done before the business can officially start.

Step 4: Set Up the Financial Accounts and Tracking Systems. Instead of operating your child's business income and expenses out of your personal family bank account, set up separate bank accounts for the business. Unless your child is in high school, they will not be able to have their own checking account to manage their business income and expenses. Instead you may have to open up a custodial checking or savings account with both your name and their name on the account. Call around to several different banks and credit unions to find out what the best options are and which have the lowest fees.

Every business needs to track income and expenses to have proper accounting for tax reporting purposes. Though your child will not need to file taxes unless they have made more than $600 in income from their business, it is still a good idea to start tracking income and expenses from day one so that they can see how the business is growing. This can be done in a simple paper ledger or on a simple computer program like Excel or something more detailed such as Quick Books.

Step 5: Get the Business Branding Completed and Order Promotional Materials. Every business needs a great logo and other branding that sets it apart from all the other businesses in the market. This logo can be designed by your child or by a company such as Logo Nerds. Once you have decided on a logo for the company, promotional materials can be ordered. There are many companies to choose from when it comes to ordering business cards, sticker, pens and such. We have always used Vista Print as they provide inexpensive products and fast delivery. Keep in mind that for security purposes you will not want to disclose your home address or phone number on your child's business cards. Instead, consider setting up a free Google Voice number to list on the business cards. The Google Voice account can forward all calls to a different number and can also be used to return phone calls to customers and so forth. We also recommend setting up PO Box to handle all business mail so that you don't have to give your home address out to anyone.

Step 6: Begin Marketing and Advertising. There is no need to wait until the business cards come in to start marketing and creating buzz about the business. Start telling friends and family right away and ask them to tell their friends and family too. Step a Facebook Fanpage and start getting people to "LIKE" the page. Another way to market is through a website. Nearly every young entrepreneur that we interviewed has a website so be sure to check out their sites for great ideas. There are companies that offer free websites, but if you want a custom site that has a unique name, you will want to purchase your own domain name and website hosting. Other great ways to market are networking events such as Tweetups, Meetups, BNI and Chamber of Commerce lunches. Just remember that when your mouth is open, your business is open! Start offering your products and services to others in a pleasant and positive way.

Step 7: Sell, Serve and Follow-Up. The next step in the process is to actually sell your products or services. Once you sell something and offer great customer service, you begin the process of following-up to develop a life-long client. Customers who are happy with the product or service will come back to again and again. They will also likely tell their friends and family about you. Use a simple notebook or a computer program to track customers and what they have purchased. This will allow you to follow-up effectively. If you have a website, be sure that you get your clients name and email entered into a database program such as Mail Chimp, a service that is free if your customer database is under 2,000.

As you taken action on the Seven Steps, you may also consider the other supplemental courses on our site that will help you at various stages of the business such as:

Press Forward: This course gives great insight on ways to grow your business through free and low cost traditional media outlets such as radio, TV, newspapers, magazines and press releases. The course covers do-it-yourself approaches to getting lots of press. In our first year online, Jacob was featured in http://Forbes.com and many other blogs and local newspapers. Clarissa was featured in several foodie blogs and local news outlets for her cookbook, and Raising CEO Kids has been featured on television, in http://YahooFinance.com, http://Reuters.com, international blogs, dozens of radio shows and local newspapers. All of the free press was made possible implementing the same strategies taught in the course Press Forward.

Social Media LiFT makes sense of using social networking for business purposes. It covers tips and tools for properly using Facebook, Twitter, LinkedIn, and Youtube to grow your business. In the course you will gain understanding on how to meet people from around the world as well as get market feedback on business products and services. In Social Media 101, you will learn how to attract and sell to customers as well as generate buzz about your products and services in a way that is engaging and fun. Security issues for kids as well as parents are also addressed so that everyone stays safe in cyber space.

Outsourcing 101 teaches you how to delegate to others so you can live your life and still get more done. You will understand and implement the process of breaking your business up into tasks and defining what can only be done by you and what tasks can be done by others. You will learn how to create easy-to-follow task instructions so that each task can be given to someone else to do. Course attendees will understand where to find people to delegate to, how to hire and communicate with them as well as how to track progress of tasks. Outsourcing 101 is so effective and simple for business owners that even our kids now delegate certain tasks in their businesses.

There are many other courses on http://RaisingCEOKids.com, so be sure to look in our courses section for dates and times that those are offered. Some are even offered as home-study options so that you can take them at your own pace in the convenience of your home.

QUESTIONS FOR REFLECTION

1. What steps can you take today to help your child get started in business?
2. Are there steps that will require more investigation before you can complete them and if so have you set a time on your calendar to assist your child in the investigation process?

THE FUTURE

It's hard to predict the future, and sometimes looking forward can give us a great deal of anxiety. Taking steps to prepare now can allow for opportunities to open up down the road.

Your CEO Kid may or may not be considering college, and in today's global economy a degree is not always necessarily required to be successful. However, taking steps right now to prepare for college allows that opportunity to stay open. Not preparing could close that door altogether. To prepare, your CEO Kid can investigate *with* you to determine which schools have the programs they are interested in, and perhaps which ones strongly support entrepreneurship.

They can also start tracking all of the things that they do for charity, as well as everywhere they speak, and all of their media pieces, whether print, radio, online, or TV. This can be a full-time job in and of itself if your child becomes a "media darling" like some of the CEO Kids we interviewed, so set up a spreadsheet to track all of it and update it as the media comes in. We strongly suggest you consider creating a digital or online résumé to track all of the charity and business work, too. It is easy to quickly add to your digital résumé. Also anyone looking to hire you will find what they need quickly instead of having to request the résumé from you.

As business grows, and depending on the liability associated with the business, necessary legal and tax issues will need to be addressed. Legal issues such as the identity of the company, whether it is a sole proprietorship, partnership, LLC, S-Corp, or other business formation, will need to be looked at. If intellectual property management or patents need to be obtained; that also will take some time and preparation so that they are handled in the present as well as taken care of in the future.

QUESTIONS FOR REFLECTION

1. What opportunities do you see as possibilities in the future for you or your CEO Kid?

2. What things can you put in place today or in the near future to ensure that those opportunities are available to you or your CEO Kid down the road?

9

SOCIETY'S ROLE

The accomplishments generated by youth entrepreneurs and their families largely stem from their own vision, hard work, and impermeable attitude. But we also recognize that one of the primary barriers for youth entrepreneurship is the policies that influence employment (in general and among youth), academic achievement, and the ability to balance work and family. When proper policies are in place, we will see more youth entrepreneurs—and they will experience greater success. Society, families, and communities will benefit from youth who have purpose, know how to work and love to work, and who have a positive attitude toward their accomplishments.

We formally call upon policy makers, wherever they are and in whatever their capacity, to develop a sense of vision as to what our world can be like when youth are given the opportunity to succeed. We applaud policies and people that encourage employment among youth, and know that these programs take time, money, and effort. Programs that successfully match young people with potential employers and mentors serve as particularly meaningful transition structures for youth, and can help youth assimilate into a larger, more productive community.

Within these youth-to-work programs, we encourage teachers and other educators to promote entrepreneurship among their students. Entrepreneurial activities are especially meaningful for adolescents because it is a period of exploration and struggle for independence and expression. The reality is that young people are more familiar with technology and social media than adults, and given the proper education, can make a strong foundation for their own futures by following their dreams.

Carolyn Montgomery, mother of Michael Montgomery, founder of Double-Take Industries, said,

> I think we were extraordinarily lucky to live in a town that offers things like Business Professionals of America, internships with local government, and youth organizations such as Emmett Young Entrepreneurs Club and Youth Action Counsel.

There is still the strong ideology that exists within the academic framework that a child must do well in school, and into college, in order to be a successful, happy adult. We certainly do not want to discourage school achievement but recommend that we continually assess whether—and how— to create an environment in which those with other talents and interests can still find a path toward success. We recommend youth entrepreneurial classes and clubs, so that youth can discuss similar interests, strategies, and identify mentors. We also strongly recommend that parents get involved in learning about entrepreneurship. Even if you do not know anything about business, you can learn alongside your kids. Together you can create successful businesses and learn to turn passion and gifts into products and services that the market wants and needs.

Expanding entrepreneurial clubs, organizations, and business incubators into college serves as a win-win for both the entrepreneur and the college. We were excited to learn that these programs are rapidly increasing. One example of this is Matthew Turcotte, author and founder of North Shore Solutions, who is attending college—and his program will help build his business as part of his schooling by giving access to free office space, interns, and advisors.

Politicians can find ways for promoting legislation that improves the entrepreneurial spirit of youth. It's definitely not easy to balance one's beliefs, values, and limited funds with what is "right" for everyone. But, despite the fact that youth do not vote, they impact our society in countless ways. Who will work in order to pay for our Social Security benefits? Who will pave the roads? Who will work in or own the stores we will need to shop in? Who will be the leaders in our businesses or communities when we become aged and dependent upon them?

We also call upon faith-based and community institutions to promote greater youth entrepreneurship and charity, and we encourage them to determine whether their strategies lead to successful outcomes for youth. We appreciate the hard work and volunteerism that goes into Boy Scouts, Girl Scouts, Boys and Girls Club, Big Brother and Big Sister organizations, churches, and many others, including those we have listed in our Resource list. We know there are many others, and want you to know that your work is valued.

Another avenue for reducing the barriers is in the banking industry, where various policies limit or exclude youth from owning their own business checking accounts (in some states). We understand the purpose of such legislation, in that it protects youth from being responsible for writing bad checks, but we believe it sends the wrong message to young people and their parents. When parents feel their children are knowledgeable and responsible enough, they should be able to make the choice as to when their children can open their own business checking account. Banks could still hold collateral (i.e. parent's account, stocks/bonds) if the youth failed to manage the finances appropriately, and parents serve as a backup so that banks will not lose money in the process.

We are passionate about youth entrepreneurship and raising CEO Kids, as evidenced in this book and the more than 500 articles on our website (written in just over a year). We know that if you are a parent, you want your kids to be successful, and we know that even if you haven't owned a business, you are capable of helping your child or children to be successful in business.

The following pages contain brief bios of kids who are or were just like our kids and your kids. Read their bios. Go to their websites. Be inspired by what they have accomplished and what they continue to accomplish. Then— TAKE ACTION! Do something every single day to assist your child in becoming a successful entrepreneur, whether it is for profit, for a cause, or both.

Meet the CEO Kids
and
Young Entrepreneurs

Adora Svitak
adorasvitak.com

Author, teacher, and speaker Adora Svitak has sold thousands of books, presented to hundreds of classrooms, and spoken at dozens of conferences. The internationally influential thirteen year old has had her first book, *Flying Fingers*, published in China, Vietnam, and Britain, and her witty and engaging free teaching videos have been watched around the world.

Adora advocates for many causes, including youth empowerment, children's rights, education equality and reform, and ending world hunger. In February of 2011, she received the National Education Association Foundation's Award for Outstanding Service to Public Education, an award previously given to recipients like Billie Jean King and Mr. Rogers. Though she may not stand quite as tall, eventually she hopes to have a list of accomplishments just as long.

Alanna Meyers
bandage-remover.com

Eight-year-old Alanna Meyers, inventor of Taking Off™, an organic and natural-source "Pain-Free Bandage Remover", has received national attention for her remarkable bandage-removing product, with interviews on the popular television shows "The Doctors" and "Rachel Ray". She has also been interviewed by ABC News, (Tampa, FL), *Destinations Safety Harbor Magazine*, and University of South Florida, regarding its Young Inventors Contest. Alanna is a remarkable young lady who attends a Montessori Academy and is in the third grade. She excels in school, tennis, piano, art, theater, and languages.

Alex Hodara
hodararealestate.com

Alex Hodara is one of *Businessweek*'s 2010 "Top 25 Entrepreneurs Under 25," a recent graduate from Boston University's School of Management, and the founder of America's first student-owned and operated real estate brokerage (as coined by CNBC and the Association of Realtors). An entrepreneur from an early age, Alex successfully created and ran several successful businesses, including a poker chip-importing company and the eBoy Charity Foundation. Since starting Hodara Real Estate Group, Alex has put $15 million of real estate under agreement.

Allyson Ames
wonderlandbakery.com

Allyson Ames is president and founder of Wonderland Bakery. She turned her passion for baking, which started at age five, into an authentic lifestyle brand for the young, young at heart, and anyone with a sweet tooth. Wonderland Bakery focuses on enchantingly delicious and whimsically fun desserts, parties, and products that are centered around the family baking experience. Allyson Ames was featured in the Top 10 Personal Brands by *Entrepreneur* magazine, Entrepreneur of the Year by the National Association of Women Business Owners (NAWBO), and an *Inc.* magazine Top 5000 List recipient.

Amanya Pavelka
4realkids.com

Amanya Pavelka, age ten, has owned various ventures since the age of six. She currently owns A's Sunflower Seed Co., which sells South Dakota farm-fresh sunflower seeds. She first "discovered" these wonderful-tasting seeds after visiting her grandparents in the summer—the seeds are grown and manufactured on a farm ten miles from her grandparents' farm. And now she is the only distributor in her state!

Andrew Hill
rumfordaquatics.com

Andrew Hill began serious entrepreneurial endeavors as he started high school in 2006. Now a student at Arizona State University's W.P. Carey School of Business, he is the co-president of the entrepreneurship club at Arizona State University. The club's mission is to provide entrepreneurs education outside the classroom and bring in entrepreneurs to share their experiences with members of the club. Currently Andrew is working on Rumford Aquatics, an aquascaping (planted aquarium) supply company. Other ventures are in the planning stages; he does not plan to stop at just one. He is passionate about education, and has also been a member of CollegeBoard's Advisory Panel on Student Concerns. He believes that entrepreneurship and education are the two key areas that can change humanity for the better, and he aims to help make that happen by promoting education and entrepreneurship.

Aneesha Raghunathan
hopelinefashions.org

Aneesha Raghunathan was seventeen when she started Hope Line Fashions Inc., a nonprofit that empowers women all over the world. She started the organization to help the women she saw working in sweatshop conditions, believing that they deserved a better life and a chance to follow their dreams. The organization has gone above and beyond her expectations, becoming international, hiring twenty women to make shirts, selling hundreds worldwide, distributing textbooks and supplies to impoverished schools, and providing thousands of dollars as start-up capital, scholarships, and aid to the women and girls that are our future.

Anshul Samar
elementeo.com

Anshul Samar is the CEO and founder of Alchemist Empire, Inc. and the creator of The Elementeo Game, a chemistry card game that helps students explore chemistry through gaming. In Elementeo, element cards like Oxygen Life-Giver and Sodium Dragon have their own personality and battle with each other using properties and oxidation states—players create compounds, combat with element reactions, and conquer their opponents with black holes and slippery bases. Anshul began prototyping and building Elementeo in sixth grade and launched it during his first year of high school, incorporating his company and learning about working with artists, manufacturers, and lawyers on the way.

Anshul has given talks at the National Academies of Sciences, National Association of Gifted Children's Conference, and the Maker Faire, and has also been featured in the *New York Times*, Scholastic News, and PBS *BizKids*. Today, Elementeo sells in select stores across the country, including the MIT Museum Store, Exploratorium, and amazon.com. Kids, parents, and scientists enjoying playing and learning chemistry. In fact, after Anshul and Dr. Tom Lane, the president of the American Chemical Society, had an Elementeo match, Dr. Lane bought fifty games!

Asya Gonzalez
Wix.com/stinkyfeetgurlz/
stinkyfeetgurlz

Asya Gonzalez is the fourteen-year-old founder, creator, and designer of Stinky Feet Gurlz, a 1940s-inspired apparel line of sassy and quirky characters. She is also the founder of She Is Worth It, a foundation and cause to bring awareness and action to the atrocities of human trafficking, more specifically, child sex trafficking. Asya has a love for creativity, and when she's not working on her designs or at school, you can find her strumming on her acoustic guitar, spiking a volleyball, or laughing her head off with good friends and family.

Austin Evers
appuous.com

Austin Evers is a young entrepreneur and technology enthusiast from Atlanta, Georgia. The company, Appuous, Inc., which he founded in 2009, develops software applications for iOS and Mac OS X platforms. Since the age of nine, Austin has had the goal of owning and operating his own business. He intends to pursue his passion for business by working to improve operations, enhance growth, and increase profitability in his current and future endeavors.

Autumn Miller
aspenviewstudios.com

Autumn Miller came to the coffee business naturally. Out of her seven siblings, she was the one who would follow Daddy onto the porch of their mountain home as he roasted his small batches of coffee. She was sipping as early as allowed and quickly developed a taste for good, fresh coffee. Family friends asking to take coffee home led her to roasting on her own and making sales. Now she sells at local fairs and events, provides coffee for her father's business events, and makes individual sales.

Becca Doll

Becca Doll has been a Girl Scout since kindergarten. As a Junior Girl Scout, she wanted to earn her Silver Award. While trying to decide what to do for her project, she realized she wanted to help children, and that's when she came across an organization called KidsCan. KidsCan helps families that have kids with cancer. With the donation of 200 duffle bags, she was able to get started, and used grant money and money she had earned selling Girl Scout cookies to purchase material to make 200 tie blankets. Becca also spent several months making blankets, and she bought art supplies, books, and games and placed them in bags for kids with cancer. Other companies and businesses throughout the state donated items to help fill the bags. After all of the work was done, she gave the bags to KidsCan. The bags now get handed out to children throughout the state when they find out they have cancer. Becca hopes that each bag handed out gives the kids something to smile about.

Becca Robison
astrotots.org

Becca Robison started her venture while still in elementary school. AstroTots, Space Camp for Little Dippers, has reached thousands of underserved girls ages four to ten around the world. Through crafts and experiments, she helps excite girls about science and encourages science education in the young people she serves. The sustainability of this project was made possible by grants from Youth Service America, Youth Venture, Yahoo, and other organizations that support youth empowerment. Now in its ninth year, AstroTots has goals to continue its global outreach to countries where education for girls is not a priority. Becca feels like education changes lives and wants to use AstroTots to inspire girls everywhere to reach for the stars.

Ben Johnson
runningwildpaintball.com

BBen Johnson and his brothers started Running Wild Paintball, Inc. when Ben was fourteen years old. Ben played paintball on a semi-pro level at the age of eleven. He and his brothers loved the game and they wanted to take it to the next step so they started their own field. This was no small endeavor, and with a heavy burden of work the venture is slowly starting to pay off. Ben is now graduating high school and planning on attending SUNY Geneseo for biology, then off to med school. He has no intentions of closing his business while in college. Hence the appropriate name of Running Wild.

Benjamin Jacques
meltingwaves.com

Benjamin Jacques is a nineteen-year-old designer who makes a full-time living online in the graphic design industry. He has been designing for companies around the world since he was fifteen years old. Ironically, his elementary school teacher told him he wasn't "very artistic," and that moment changed his life, as he invested his time and energy into learning about graphic design. Starting in middle school, he won various awards for his new talent. Benjamin now has fifteen clients spread across five countries, and has a website that teaches designers how to set up a business, market it, and how to generate profit from it.

Benjamin Lang
epiclaunch.com

Benjamin Lang is the founder of EpicLaunch.com, a popular blog for young entrepreneurs. He started an eBay business at age fourteen and did so well he was featured on Channel 12. Ben is currently working on http://myschoolhelp.com, a place for high school students to find their classmates' notes and reviews.

Bradley Ericson
www.3secondreceipts.com

Bradley Ericson is an aspiring entrepreneur and zealous undergraduate student majoring in business administration with a dual concentration in marketing and entrepreneurship at Drexel University. Bradley is ranked as the top National College Entrepreneur of 2009 by *Entrepreneur* magazine. He co-founded 3SecondReceipts LLC with his mentor and older brother, Timothy Ericson. 3SecondReceipts aims to solve the inconveniences caused by paper receipts by developing a solution that enables digital receipts. Bradley expects nothing less than perfection and a positive attitude in his academic, athletic, and professional endeavors. He lives by the famous quote by Emerson: "Nothing great was ever achieved without enthusiasm." Aside from his professional endeavors, Bradley is one of the top business students at Drexel University and an avid golfer, field hockey player, and fencer.

Brandi Thomas
ballroombybrandi.com

Brandi Thomas began ballroom dancing at age nine with her grandfather, just to pass the time. The two of them gave demonstrations promoting ballroom dance, and for several years Brandi volunteered teaching ballroom dance to students and adults. At age sixteen, she petitioned USA Dance, the national organization for ballroom athletes, to be allowed to teach for profit. It was then that Ballroom By Brandi became a reality. Brandi is an exceptional choreographer. She specializes in the first dance for the bride and groom, choreographs for LSU Ballroom Dance Club and Tiger Dancesport, and continues to compete.

Brendon Maxwell
utopiancoffee.com

Brendon Maxwell began his first venture at sixteen, selling Dum Dum Pops® to his high school peers. What started as a way to be challenged and make a few extra dollars from the bulk section of the grocery store quickly grew to buying the delicious treats in boxes of 2,400, keeping margins, and "hiring" others. After several more successful summer companies, including selling imported goods out of a truck, painting house numbers on curbs, and a car detailing/estate management company, he co-founded Utopian Coffee Co. in 2006, which has been roasting and delivering extraordinary coffee throughout the U.S. More importantly, UtopianCoffee.com has been positively impacting international communities in coffee-growing regions, giving back to the people and land that provide this incredible product.

Brett Wells
brettonthenet.com

Brett Wells got his entrepreneurial start at the age of ten when he opened Brett's Snack Shack to provide snacks, drinks, and even painted rocks to the neighbors. He turned a tidy profit and even made it a point to donate to his favorite charity, Save the Manatees. Now a teenager, Brett is learning about Internet marketing and social media and hopes to parlay his newfound skills to future online business ventures.

Caleb Miller
aspenviewstudios.com

LLiving in an Aspen stand in the Rocky Mountains provided the perfect venue for Caleb Miller to start his woodworking craft. Inspired by his father's hobby of making Aspen furniture and accessories for their home, Caleb started making his own lamps, coasters, and candles to sell at local fairs and events and to family and friends. Today he fills large Christmas orders and is working toward buying a car with his earnings.

Cassidy McVey
minkydrawstringbags.yolasite.com

Cassidy McVey knows a great deal about the wonderful world of crafts—from colorful hair clips adorned with flowers and cozy drawstring bags to hold your prized possessions to frilly tutus and everything in between. Cassidy learned about sewing from her grandparents, which helped her propel her business on the Internet. Cassidy has a great mindset and enjoys school and participating in sports.

Chelsea Eubank
faithfulfish.com

The story of how Faithful Fish was founded is an American entrepreneurial story of Chelsea Eubank, who became successful despite many personal losses and challenges. At seventeen Chelsea saw a niche in the Christian clothing market that was not being addressed and that was the beginning of her clothing line called Faithful Fish. She was inspired to create the line after experiencing five personal losses in her family over a two-year period, including the loss of her father while on the phone with her. With renewed faith, Chelsea wanted to wear something that subtly showed her faith and was both trendy and classic. After looking in stores and even going on eBay, she was unable to find what she wanted to wear. Chelsea went on to create her own logo and line of designs.

Chelsea is an unlikely entrepreneur. She has a learning disability and went to private learning disability schools for most of her early years. She recently graduated from Beacon College in Florida, which is the only four-year accredited learning-disability college in America. She has been on FOX & Friends, Dave Ramsey's TV show, and was invited back the following week to speak about entrepreneurship on Dave Ramsey's radio show. In addition, Chelsea is an inspirational speaker.

Chip Lowe
cwd.me

Little did Chip Lowe know that a website he designed in sixth grade would lead him to the success he has created today. Chip founded CWD in 2002 as "Chip's Web Design". He had a vision for his business to grow to include all aspects of technology, and in 2004 he expanded CWD to video services, including video filming, editing, and DVD production. Chip continues to grow and expand his business and now offers services that include web design, video, social networking development, event planning, technical coordination, online stores, marketing, hosting services, and more.

Chris Gross
ChrisGross.net

Chris Gross is a self-taught Internet and web page guru who continues to expand his horizons. He started learning about computers at the age of 10 and was programming websites for local businesses by the age of 12. Chris was home schooled and used his time wisely between classes. He has been the sole designer behind his sister's, (Mary Sarah Gross) web presence and will continue in that role. He has also become an expert in the area of social media and entertainment websites. In the last year, Chris reached his childhood dream of becoming a specialist at the local Apple store. Combining his set of skills, passion for Apple Products, and his love of people, he has been a great success!

133

Chris Hughes
brainsmartsuccess.com

Young entrepreneur Chris Hughes is known as the Juggling Entrepreneur by all of his clients and on the web. He juggles a variety of businesses along with balls, clubs, and other things. Chris is currently the Internet marketer behind Brain Smart Success. Brain Smart Success is a company that is all about finding and using the smartest ways to build businesses. Their main focus is helping older business owners learn how they can use the Internet to market their business.

Christian Pavelka
starfishsoap.webs.com

Christian Pavelka, age fourteen, is a thinking entrepreneur who only invests time and money after evaluating risks carefully. He has thoughtfully owned businesses since the age of six, starting with family puppet shows and various lemonade stands on the corner and in the local park. He started Starfish Soap Co. in 2007, and is currently building Christian's Guitar Studio, where he offers group guitar lessons in a playing-based method.

Clarissa Cook
creatingwithcc.com

Clarissa Cook, twelve, is the founder of Creating with CC and author of *Cooking with CC: Sweet Treats and Bake Sale Secrets*, which has been featured on numerous foodie blogs and in newspapers. Clarissa is a social entrepreneur who gives much of her profits to Keaton Raphael Memorial, a nonprofit group the helps kids with cancer. She enjoys sewing and has made and donated her blankets to the children of Haiti.

Clinton Skakun
clintonskakun.com

Clinton Skakun is a twenty-year-old entrepreneur who started his first web design company with his dad at the age of fifteen. He's spent his teens exploring numerous business opportunities, facing challenges, and learning by trial and error. Aside from writing Entrepreneurs-Guide.com, working a night job, and building websites, he's also currently in the groundworks of a new online start-up called Rent2Bike.com, a web-based service that helps tourists find the right bicycle rentals.

After reading countless books on business and being around successful business people, Clinton says, "Doing your best and working harder than than 'the pack' is critical to success in business and life." He goes on to add, "It's hard to beat the person who puts in extra hours. Even if you think you have the so-called 'secrets.'" If there's one thing his parents have instilled in him, it's that there are no four-hour work weeks to success.

Cole Spradlin
facebook.com/GrassmanLawnCare

Cole Spradlin has been a dreamer for years! He dreams of playing collegiate sports, launching businesses, and inventing, as well as moving to Australia and traveling abroad. Many kids dream, but very few have the ability to dream and execute. Cole is fortunate to have both dreaming and execution firmly planted in his DNA. He has launched a lawn business called GrassMan Lawn Care in Steamboat Springs, CO, that is growing, and he has several inventions that he is working on and hopes to unleash soon.

Connell Wise
usyouthchamber.com

Connell Wise is the founder and CEO of the U.S. Youth Chamber of Commerce—"The World's 1st Chamber of Commerce For 13–25 Year Old Business Executives and Social Change Makers." Despite living with ADD, second-degree heart blockage, Asthma, and Type II Diabetes, Connell has been a youth rights advocate for the past six years and has brought his beliefs of youth involvement in government to both local and national levels. In several capacities, Connell has worked for the District of Columbia government as a government commissioner over the Executive Office of The Mayor Office of Volunteerism, as well as his work as a President Barack Obama campaign fellow. Previous to this, Connell founded CWBN (Connell Wise Broadcasting Network), an online news website that gives teens a place to report what is happening in their community and offers a forum to discuss how they feel about it.

Currently Connell is in his second year as a double major at Curry College, studying business management with a concentration in nonprofit management and a communication concentration in television production/digital video. Connell is an active member of the Community Emergency Response Team in Washington, D.C. and the U.S. Medical Reserve Corp.

Cory Levy
corylevy.com

Cory Levy is the co-founder and COO of One, Inc. One is a venture-financed company with a mobile application that notifies you when there are people around you with similar interests. Think of it as a way to ask everyone you pass hundreds of questions and get notified if they answer yes enough times. Prior to One, Cory co-founded three companies, including a sports memorabilia company, a T-shirt printing company, and an entrepreneurial education start-up with a Duke professor. Over the last few years he has interned at TechStars, Union Square Ventures, The Founders Fund, and DFJ Mercury.

Crystal Yan
crystalcyan.com
hereswhatsnext.com

Crystal C. Yan is eighteen years old and co-produced *What's Next: 25 Big Ideas from Gen-Yers Under 25*, a book featuring youth writers from Seattle to Sierra Leone. She also co-founded the Social Startup Summit, a social entrepreneurship boot camp for middle and high school students. When she's not doing graphic design work (clients include literacy nonprofits and medical schools) or blogging, she enjoys speaking at conferences and schools, dance (Bollywood, tango, Kuchipudi), making jewelry, and origami.

Dakota Lee
DakotaLee.com

Dakota Lee was just in fourth grade when she began to write her very own book. At the time, Dakota and her mom, Mary-Ellen, weren't thinking of making it into a book, it was just something to do. But as the nine-year-old girl progressed in her writing and the pages kept adding up, publishing her book seemed imminent. In 2007, Dakota Lee published her very first book, titled *Flash of Freedom*, and has since sold close to 1,000 copies of it. She has also spoken to well over 1,000 children and adults about the passion to write. Now Dakota is fifteen years old and has just entered high school. She has big plans for the future and intends to keep writing novels, as well as venture into nonfiction and acting. The future is looking bright for this teenage entrepreneur.

Dale Stephens
dalejstephens.com
uncollege.org

At age eleven, Dale Stephens started his first business, Creekside Cards and Photos, through which he sold his photography. This venture led him to serve as the photographer for Gavin Newsom's Gubernatorial Campaign. At seventeen he went to UCLA for the Academy of Business Leadership and wrote a business plan for a low-cost transatlantic airline. A year later he immersed himself in entrepreneurship by creating a position at Zinch in San

Francisco, an education start-up that connects more than 2.5 million high school students with more than 850 colleges and graduate schools worldwide. He is now leading the UnCollege movement, a new model for self-directed higher education created out of frustrations with his college experience. UnCollege has garnered national media attention, and at only nineteen years old he's been featured in the *Chronicle of Higher Education*, ABC, and *The Huffington Post*.

Dallas Crilley
kidpreneurclub.com

Dallas Crilley is a budding entrepreneurial superstar and much-sought-after motivational speaker. After he finishes his homework, you can usually find him out speaking to groups of all ages on how to inspire the next generation to greatness. He's the author of *Kidpreneur: Genius Ways for Kids to Pay Their Way Through College*, a book he wrote when he was just fifteen years old. He also runs a successful designer T-shirt and bracelet company, which he uses to raise money for cancer research.

Instead of "It's never too late", Dallas believes "It's never too early!" Michael Dell started Dell computers from his college dorm room. Mark Zuckerberg created Facebook while still a student at Harvard. Both are now billionaires. And Dallas plans to follow in their entrepreneurial footsteps.

Dallas Goodwin
dallasdesigns.artfire.com

While trying to earn spending money at age six, Dallas Goodwin quickly realized that working for someone else was not as rewarding as she had hoped. She wondered how she could make money doing something she enjoyed. And that's when Dallas Designs was born. Dallas started out designing custom gift bags and selling them at local shops and to friends. She now creates jewelry and accessories and sells them locally and online.

Danette M. Nixon
princessjewels4kids.com

Danette M. Nixon, also known as "The Youth Success Princess", is an author, speaker, and youth entrepreneur. She operates a successful business designing sterling silver jewelry for kids and is an up-and-coming fashion designer. Danette is the creator of "How to Start a Business—Just for Kids" video presentation used to introduce elementary age kids to the world of business; "Know Your Dough Game Show", a six-week webinar class that teaches tweens about money; and is currently working on a new book. She is also the co-facilitator of "The Bookbag Entrepreneur Club", a program designed to support the business growth of youth entrepreneurs from twelve to eighteen years old.

Daniel Wetter
about.me/danielwetter

Daniel Wetter is a journalist who just happens to be in high school. He started reporting as a *Scholastic News* Kids Press Corps reporter in 2008, covering everything from the 2010 Winter Olympics in Vancouver to the H1N1 epidemic. He is currently a freelance video journalist reporting for the *Roseville Press Tribune* and the *Sacramento Bee*. Daniel covered the Galleria Mall fire in October 2010, which earned recognition from Gold Country Media. He has also started up a broadcast news outlet at his school, Roseville High School. He is always on the hunt for good stories and strives to be the best reporter he can be.

David Garbera
khsmilers.co.uk
garberaenterprise.co.uk

David Garbera has successfully combined his business interests with his academic studies, and is currently studying medicine at the University of Liverpool (UK). Garbera Enterprise was incorporated as a means of publishing and marketing a trilogy of books encouraging young people to take on the challenge of starting their own business. David has received several entrepreneurial awards, including the "Most Enterprising Student" award at the University of Liverpool, the "Young Entrepreneur of the Year 2010." He was selected by the university and the National Council for Graduate Entrepreneurship to deliver a webinar to graduates looking to start their own business.

David King
davidbeking.com

David King started forming the mindset of an entrepreneur after reading the book *Rich Dad, Poor Dad* by Robert Kiyosaki. His first job was a paper route while he was young, then he began delivering newspapers for the bigger well-known newspapers seven days a week. He later started working from home and launched his first information product called "twitter influence." He has created and sold additional products since then. David now markets his products and business through the Internet and various forms of online marketing.

David Wilkinson
optank.com

In 2006, David Wilkinson started his first online business at the age of twelve. Today he runs a network of half a dozen or so sites, from the nonprofit OpTank.com online "think tank" to more business-oriented services, such as SwapLike.com, a Facebook marketing platform. David also invests in seed-stage web apps and runs a closed-door consulting group.

Derek Johnson
thederekjohnson.com

Derek Johnson started businesses when he was very young, but his real success came in October 2007, when he founded Tatango, an angel-backed company originally named networkText. Initially started as a solution for his fraternity (Delta Upsilon) to communicate with fraternity brothers, Tatango has since grown to become one of the industry leaders in the mobile marketing space. Tatango works with a broad spectrum of clients ranging from small to Fortune 500 businesses.

Donny Ouyang
kinkarso.com

Donny Ouyang is a young Canadian entrepreneur with a passion for doing business online. In 2005, Donny began exploring online business by developing and investing in websites and web applications. In 2007, Kinkarso Tech Ltd. was formed to house these projects under a common brand. Donny is known for being able to increase the value of websites quickly and cost effectively. Since the formation of Kinkarso Tech, Donny has been featured in numerous newspaper articles, websites, magazines, television, radio, and books. He is a winner of the 2010 Global Student Entrepreneur Awards. Today, Donny manages Kinkarso Tech and its branched startups as CEO.

Drew DeLeon
aktivewrap.com
At the age when most girls are playing with Barbies and watching cartoons, ten-year-old Drew DeLeon had bigger ideas. Her advanced organizational skills, coupled with being a natural leader with the desire to earn extra money, sparked her dream to have her own business. With the support of her parents, Drew decided to go for it—never allowing her young age to put limitations on her dreams. She started her business, AktiveWrap, and sells rolls of colored foam prewrap to young female athletes who need to hold their hair during sports activities. Drew has been featured as a young business owner on the TV show *Young Icons*. And she was selected as the youngest CEO at the biggest Soccer Nation Expo in the world, from among hundreds of business owners, at the tender age of ten!

Dylan Brooks
skatepunkz.com

Dylan loves to draw and thought it would be fun to design t-shirts that he and his friends could wear. He lives in Southern California with his mom, twin brother Ethan, and his dog, Ruffus. Dylan believes in giving back and donates a portion of every sale to the Brittany Foundation, a nonprofit charity dedicated to the rescue, rehabilitation, care and placement of homeless dogs.

Eliana de Las Casas
elianacooks.com

Ten-year-old kid chef Eliana de Las Casas grew up in a family of cooks. With grandparents from the Philippines, Cajun Louisiana, Cuba, and Honduras, Eliana's recipes have international flair. She loves spending time in the kitchen with her family. Eliana says, "Cooking is so much fun. You can be creative and invent new recipes." When asked to name her favorite food, Eliana says, "It's hard to pick a favorite because I like so many kinds of food." In the future, Eliana plans to design cookware for kids, create a line of spices, and host her own TV cooking show. She also wants to teach kids that good food is more than chicken nuggets and French fries. Eliana's first cookbook, *Eliana Cooks! Recipes for Creative Kids,* was released in October 2010. Visit Eliana's website and watch her video cooking tutorials for kids. Her motto is, "Cool kids cook and get creative in the kitchen!"

Emil Motycka
motyckalawns.com

At thirteen-years-old, Emil took out his first loan: $8000 to purchase a commercial lawn mower. He paid off his four-year loan in two years. It was the beginning of Motycka Enterprises, LLC, a holding company with businesses that offer everything from building and janitorial maintenance to lawn care, tree care, snow removal, and even Christmas light installation. The company helped Emil to earn $250,000 his senior year of college and be named one of America's Coolest College Startups by *Inc.* magazine.

Emil is currently a senior at the University of Colorado's Leeds School of Business in Boulder, Colorado, majoring in marketing and economics.

Emily-Anne Rigal
westophate.org

Emily-Anne Rigal is the seventeen-year-old founder of WeStopHate.org, a nonprofit program created to promote "teen-esteem" (self-esteem in teens) through the power of online videos and social media. Emily-Anne is better known as @Schmiddlebopper in the online world and is always seen wearing a pink bow headband. She loves New York (but just as friends!) and believes that imagination is stronger than knowledge. Her goal each day is simple: to be happier than a bird with a French fry!

Eric Glustrom
experienceeducate.org

Eric Glustrom is the founder and executive director of Educate!, an organization that develops the next generation of leaders and entrepreneurs in Africa who will solve poverty, disease, violence, and environmental degradation. Eric started Educate! eight years ago at age seventeen in Kyangwali Refugee Settlement, Uganda. Eric works closely with the first Educate! students who have started a successful community organization that is working to bridge the tribal divide in the Democratic Republic of Congo.

Eric and Educate! have received numerous awards and recognition, which are a testament to the potential of the youth Educate! works with: The Echoing Green Fellowship, Ashoka's Changemakers Champions of Quality Education in Africa, *Entrepreneur* magazine's 100 Brilliant Companies of 2009, and features in *Fast Company* and numerous other media outlets.

Eric graduated from Amherst College in Massachusetts in 2007, where he studied biochemistry and neuroscience. He likes skiing of all kinds, discussing social change, and is reportedly very good at catching food in his mouth.

Erin Johnson
flipoutz.com

Erin Johnson, along with her siblings, were the first youth entrepreneurs on ABC's *SharkTank*, to showcase their Flipoutz business. Erin is currently a high-school senior majoring in musical theater at Interlochen Arts Academy in Interlochen, Michigan. She has performed in local theater since the age of eight and looks forward to a career on the stage after college. She plays the guitar and piano and enjoys writing songs. The first coin created was Erin's design and is still a fave—"Peace through Music." Erin's belief in the need for self expression—whether you see yourself as a scientist, a musician, or a jock—led to the idea of Flipoutz coins as a means of telling the world proudly about yourself.

Ethan Thompson
jptmedia.com

Ethan Thompson is a teenage media entrepreneur and founder of Just Passing Through Media. His first entrepreneurial endeavor was doing small freelance writing jobs and forum posting for people around the globe. Then he moved on to helping filmmakers design their logos. He currently owns and operates his own media company and is working on building it into a successful enterprise. He specializes in videography and also provides several other services through third parties. He also currently works for a local online news website as advertising support. When Ethan isn't working he's usually helping with the audio visual needs at his church, helping lead a monthly Bible study with his friends, or out riding his mountain bike. His goal is to own a successful media company by the time he's twenty-one and devote his life to glorifying God in anything and everything he does.

Fraser Doherty
superjam.co.uk

Fraser Doherty started making jam with his grandmother at the age of just fourteen. After selling his homemade products door to door, at farmers' markets, and to small shops, he came up with a way of making jam 100% from fruit. Now, his SuperJam has sold millions of jars and is on the shelves of over a thousand supermarkets in the U.K., including Wal-Mart, Tesco, and Waitrose.

As well as building an incredibly successful brand that is exhibited in the National Museum of Scotland as an "Iconic Scottish Brand", Fraser has set up a charity. SuperJam hosts over a hundred free tea parties for elderly people every year. The events attract up to six hundred elderly people, who are living alone or in care, at each event.

Freddie Anne Hodges
itunes.apple.com/us/app/kid-measure/id366299318?mt=8

When she was eleven years old, Freddie Anne Hodges was rewarded for her good grades with an iPhone. That is when her mind started thinking about all the apps at her fingertips. While walking to the kitchen one day, she told her dad that her phone should measure her. Being a kid who was mildly obsessed with how tall she was growing, she wanted an app that would keep track of her height. This was the birth of the iPhone app now for sale on iTunes called KidMeasure. Coming up with this app idea was natural to her as she was raised in a family that always talked about being creative and emphasizing the value in creating something. Everything starts with an idea. Freddie Anne made hers into a venture for her future.

Gabriel Valo

Gabriel was just seventeen years old when he decided to take up the Call of an Entrepreneur. Today, Gabriel Serves as a CEO of Marketing Domination Co. helping businesses brand themselves online. His most notable accolade is the "Standard of Excellence" Award that was presented by Hezekiah Griggs III, "America's Youngest Media Mogul". Gabriel has been featured in numerous Power Talks, Entrepreneur Radio Stations and has been interviewed many times on Entrepreneurship and Success.

Garrett Miller
garrettcanhelp.com
gameoverindustries.com

Look up "digital native" in the dictionary and you will find a picture of Garrett Miller. Getting his first computer at age five, and learning his first programming language by the time he was ten, Garrett's affinity for computers always amazed his teachers and his peers. Garrett grew up in a bad neighborhood, and was even homeless a few times, but he always knew that it was all up to him to escape the life his environment would have shoveled him into. He made it to San Diego State University on scholarships, though he quickly learned college simply was not for him. Getting into network marketing with an older member of his fraternity, Garrett soon found a community of people building their businesses online. The rest, as they say, is history.
Garrett now co-owns his six-"soon-to-be-ten"-figure Internet marketing business, gives inspirational speeches, and helps people around the world to live their dreams.

George Drage
georgedrage.com

George Drage, a seventeen-year-old tech guru, is the owner of Drage Web Solutions. Possessing the ability to speak and write in Spanish and English, George sets himself apart from the competition by providing bilingual web consulting to anyone who seeks assistance with their technology needs. George also designs incredibly functional and beautiful websites for his friends, family members, and clients. He's also the go-to guy when a computer needs fixing.

Hannah Braboy
hannahbraboy.com

Hannah Braboy is a photographer out of Western Kentucky, marketing director at Latitude821.com, and a virtual assistant.

Hannah started blogging in 2006, and things kicked off from there. Between then and now, she has studied basic business skills, public relations and marketing, blogging, photography, and graphic and web design. Hannah was an official photographer and the photographer coordinator for BlissDom in early 2011.

Hannah Pavelka
4realkids.com

Hannah Pavelka, age twelve, has been a serial entrepreneur since the age of six. She is very creative and enjoys creating original, handmade products. She is an animal lover, and her very favorite business is the one she owns now: Hannah's Happy Horses and Growing Goats Co., where she boards horses and raises Boer meat goats. Hannah is currently writing two books: *My Trevor: The Story of How God Answered My Prayer for a Horse* and *Trail Ride Recipes.*

Hayleigh Scott
hayleighscherishedcharms.com

Hayleigh Scott was just five years old when she announced, "Hear I am!", letting the world know she was going to make her hearing aids stand out and shine rather than try to hide them. She created many drawings over the next few years of things she called "charms" and "tube twists." By age eight, her parents understood what she was trying to accomplish and helped her apply for a patent from the U.S. Patent Office. She then successfully opened her online store. Oticon, the oldest hearing-aid manufacturer in the world, awarded Hayleigh their "Focus on People" national award for eliminating negative stereotypes associated with being hearing impaired. Across the country, children and adults alike are celebrating their uniqueness with confidence due to her products for the hearing impaired.

Hunter Gross
projectkool.com

Almost four years after his mission started, Hunter Gross continues his quest to educate America's youth about the need to recycle and re-use products. As an eleven-year-old sixth grader, Hunter excitedly came home from school one day and told his astonished parents that "he needed to do something to fight global warming". Six months later, 20,000 washable, reusable, cotton canvas lunch bags arrived in Hunter's house and Project Kool was on its way to become one of the most empowering fundraisers in elementary schools across the country. Hunter's goal was (and still is) to "fight global warming one bag at a time".

**Jacob Cass
justcreativedesign.com**

Jacob Cass is a dedicated, passionate, and influential designer who has recently emigrated from Sydney, Australia, to New York City to pursue his career in the world of visual communication. Jacob has worked with clients such as Disney, Red Bull, Nike, and Star Wars, and although his skill set is vast, his major talents lie in the world of visual design, brand identity, brand strategy, UX design, UI development, new media design, and print design. Jacob has a thorough understanding of social media and the latest web technologies, which has allowed him to build a strong personal following of over 37,000+ Twitter followers and 28,000+ blog subscribers. You can find Jacob on one of his three websites: JustCreativeDesign.com, LogoDesignerBlog.com, and LogoOfTheDay.com.

**Jacob Cook
jakestutorials.com**

Jacob Cook, fifteen, is the founder of JakesTutorials and Tech Support. Jacob started his business endeavor early by selling Pokemon cards, moved to selling on eBay, and has fixed many computers around the world. He has been spotlighted in *Forbes* magazine for his entrepreneurial spirit, and has a high-ranked YouTube channel where he offers tech support and advice.

Jake Johnson
flipoutz.com

Jake Johnson and his siblings were the first youth entrepreneurs showcased in ABC's *Shark Tank* for their Flipoutz business. Jake is a sixth grader but is learning the business fast. His passions are flipoutz, sports, music, and acting. At age seven, he appeared in the movie *Talladega Nights—The Ballad of Ricky Bobby* as the young Ricky Bobby. He can currently be seen in Lifetime's *Army Wives* as Lucas Moran. While he has been known to "Eat, Sleep, Play Soccer" to distraction, these days his favorite coins may be "I'm with the band" or "Dance Fever."

James Scott
inspiringkidstoday.com
thetaekwondokid.com

James Scott's interest in becoming a CEO kid started at eight years old after he was awarded a black belt in Taekwondo. It helped triple his confidence and he realized that he was inspiring and helping kids and parents. He is now nine and a half years old and wants to be a CEO for real. He and his dad have been talking about business ideas since he got his black belt. Together they founded Inspiring Kids Today, a nonprofit organization that inspires kids to be their best.

Jamie Dunn
jamie-dunn.com

What began as setting up a market stall at age twelve, Jamie Dunn then went on to run five market stalls across Birmingham and was very successful by the age of fifteen. At the tender age of sixteen, Jamie secured his place in The Peter Jones National Enterprise Academy. He was as one of twenty-eight talented young entrepreneurs pooled from thousands of hopefuls from across the country. Jamie moved to London for six months and began learning the ins and outs of running a successful business. Becoming skilled in areas ranging from sales to management, Jamie graduated from the academy and felt as if he could achieve anything. He is now a philanthropist and respected professional speaker, sharing his experiences with other teenagers to inspire and motivate them to have the confidence and belief in themselves and their abilities to achieve anything they set their mind to.

Jason Kirby
therightlightphotography.com

Jason Kirby considers himself a progressive learner and appreciates the value of learning from others and takes every opportunity to share his knowledge with those that seek it. He started his entrepreneurial efforts as a teen and has since grown exponentially.

Jason currently owns and operates a photography company, The Right Light Photography, which focuses on shooting corporate events, headshots, and teaching photography classes. Jason's company has grown from something that was just a hobby into a thriving business. He is so talented that he has hundreds of people seeking to take his photography classes. Jason is also the director of vertical operations at eBoost Consulting, and is responsible for new client acquisition in different vertical markets. Jason and the eBoost team have created programs that utilize specific online marketing tools to market industry-specific businesses in a given geographic area.

Jason O'Neill
pencilbugs.com

Fifteen-year-old award-winning entrepreneur, speaker, philanthropist, and author, Jason O'Neill started his business, Pencil Bugs, at age nine with a simple pencil topper creation he made to sell at a craft fair. His accidental opportunity turned into a successful business with lots of media acclaim. At age twelve, *Forbes* named him on their Top 10 List for Role Models 18 & Under. He was the youngest to receive the Young Entrepreneur of the Year Award at age eleven and has been featured on TV shows such as PBS *BizKid$* and *The Young Icons* as well as in many print media. At fourteen, he became a published author with his first book, *Bitten by the Business Bug: Common Sense Tips for Business and Life from a Teen Entrepreneur*. Jason donates part of all proceeds to Rady Children's Hospital in San Diego, California.

Jayson Kingsbeer
kingsbeer.com

At just thirteen years of age, Jayson Kingsbeer turned his passion into a career and set out to professionally photograph his very first wedding. Three years down the track, Jayson is now the leading professional wedding photographer in his hometown of Gisborne, New Zealand, and has been featured numerous times on national television. Continually pleasing his clients and certainly not lacking drive and determination, Jayson strives for excellence and wants to continue growing his business to become one of New Zealand's top professional wedding and portrait photographers.

Jennifer Smart
jenniradio.com
jennifersmartfoundation.org

At the age of fourteen, Jennifer Smart is on her way to becoming a media mogul. She began her career in broadcasting when she was just six years old, as the youngest nationally syndicated talk radio host in the United States. At age eight, she began talking to stars on the red carpet at Hollywood movie premieres, and has interviewed more celebrities and industry insiders than anyone else her age. In 2009, she started the Jennifer Smart Foundation to assist charities and spread the message that you're never too young to give back. In 2010, Jennifer became the youngest radio station operator in the U.S., when the foundation purchased KALY AM 1240 in Albuquerque, NM, from Radio Disney. It is now airing the JENNiRADIO format, developed by

Jennifer for tweens, teens, and families. It features age-appropriate music, celebrity interviews, DVD and web site reviews, and messages about helping others.

Jessica Cervantes
popsycakes.com

When Jessica Cervantes was eight, she and her family fled difficulties in Cuba and came to the U.S. She often found comfort in her mom's new kitchen, and with Grandma's help, Jessica became an experienced baker. In 2008, she took one of her baked creations, now known as PopsyCakes™, and entered a business competition through the Network for Teaching Entrepreneurship. She won the competition against 30,000 other high school students. With the publicity that followed, Jessica has sold thousands of PopsyCakes™ throughout the U.S.

Joe Meglio
megliofitness.com

Joe Meglio is a strength and conditioning coach at the Underground Strength Gym in Edison, New Jersey. He is mentored by one of the brightest minds in the strength and conditioning industry, Zach Even-Esh. Although Joe has worked with various athletes at the high school, college, and professional level, he specializes in training baseball players. Aside from being a strength coach, Joe competed in his first powerlifting meet on December 11, 2010, and set the New Jersey state squat, deadlift, and total records in his weight class and division. He will be graduating from Fairleigh Dickinson University (FDU) in May 2011 with a bachelor's degree in entrepreneurial studies and is captain of the FDU Devils baseball team.

John Naylor
John Naylor Landscapes and
Lawn Care

John Naylor started exploring business ideas on his own early in his life. Being home schooled, he had time to allow for this. At the age of nine, he took action on his interest in leather crafts. He built his first saddle on his own at age twelve and also created a wide variety of things from personal items to horse tack. John's dad owns his own construction business, so he also spent days off from school working for him and learning the construction trade when he could. Later on he was inspired by the Christian film movement and had opportunities to work on several film sets, as well as a couple of his own. Now at age twenty-one, John runs his own business in the landscape construction industry through the summer months and tinkers on cars in his dad's shop as a hobby/business through the winter or slow months. He says, "To God be the Glory."

**Jonathan Cook
Jumpin' Jack Jon
raisingceokids.com/
jumpinjackjon**

Jonathan Cook, eight, is a fitness giant in size-four shoes. Jonathan does video reviews of fitness-related products and posts videos to motivate kids to stay healthy and eat nutritious foods. He is finishing up his first fitness book and stays active playing basketball, soccer, and baseball.

**ordan Puchinger
silverjax.com**

Twenty-one-year-old Jordan Puchinger, a Canadian entrepreneur, is founder of SilverJax, formerly Eidro Studios, and co-founder of Home Dealer Canada. He has also assisted in the start-up of several small Internet-based companies. Jordan started his first web agency at the age of fifteen. Jordan's continued success and dedication to excellence in his fast-paced industry has earned him national recognition as one of the best in the web design and development sector at the Skills Canada local, provincial, and national competition two years running.

In addition, his proficiency in all aspects of the web industry, including business development, design, systems, programming, and overall company management, made him a favorite guest speaker for students attending local colleges and universities in his hometown of Lethbridge, Alberta. Jordan has recently relocated to the beautiful city of Kelowna, British Columbia, and has joined the team of premier multimedia agency Media Button Communications Inc.

Julene Fleurmond
envibrance.com

Ever since she was a little girl, Julene Fleurmond has had an entrepreneurial mindset and melded it with her artistic passions. She dreamed up her first venture in elementary school, selling greeting cards and a magazine to teachers and classmates. Those early business buds bloomed into her current company, Envibrance Studios, which consists of an inspirational media network, a creative apparel and stationery line, and graphic design services. While still in high school, she received the Network for Teaching Entrepreneurship (NFTE) Young Entrepreneur of the Year Award, and her profile is also featured in NFTE's latest textbook for high school students.

Now in graduate school, Julene also inspires other young people to dream big and pursue entrepreneurship through her organization, Young Dreamer Enterprises, and youth motivational publication, DreamerENT.com. She firmly believes that young people can change the world and that following your childhood passions can be a spark to finding your purpose.

Juliette Brindak
missoandfriends.com

At age ten, Juliette Brindak tapped into her creative side, drawing what she referred to as "cool girls". In 2005, Miss O & Friends® was formed—the only lifestyle and socialization brand created "by girls...for girls" ages eight through fourteen, who have outgrown Barbie yet are not ready for Britney. Today, the brand Miss O & Friends® ranks #3 "Girls Only" websites worldwide; has published books (one of which features original stories written by girls), selling in bookstores nationwide; and enjoys global syndication of its "KidsCounsel" website column. Voted "Top 50 Women Who Inspire Us," (*Self Made* magazine, November 2010), Juliette is completing her undergraduate studies at Washington University in St. Louis, is a graduate of Astia "CEO Boot Camp," a finalist is EO's "Global Student Entrepreneurial Awards," (December 2011), and an invitee of the Russian Federation, participating in the International Economic Forum, St. Petersburg, Russia in June 2010.

Justice Mews

Justice Mews began his egg business in 2007, at the age of nine. What started out as a hobby with a few Easter chicks, soon flourished into a profitable undertaking. He continues to increase his flock each spring, purchasing pullet chicks that mature into laying hens in approximately six months. There is quite a demand for eggs raised from Justice's free-range happy hens. When Justice is not tending to his chicken chores, he enjoys tinkering with motorcycles and carpentry projects. He is always looking for a better way to get something done and looks forward to more creative financial endeavors.

Justin Crouch
justincrouch.com

Justin Crouch is a young visionary, who knows exactly what he wants: to have his own movie and publishing company. So at age eight, he set out to do just that by writing and publishing his first book, *Why I Love Mommies,* a book about just how special moms are. Justin is working on his second book, *Babies about the House,* and he and his older brother recently started their own motivational apparel company. In his free time, he likes to play video games, ride skateboards, play sports, hang out with his friends, and go to the movies.

Justin Sachs
jsachs.com

Justin Sachs is the president and CEO of Justin Sachs Companies, which consists of eight organizations, including his industry-leading publishing company, Motivational Press, Inc., and his international speaking tour, The Ultimate Success Tour. Justin is the author of four books, three of which have become bestsellers.

As one of the top leadership and peak performance speakers in the world, Justin's authentic, powerful, and inspirational presentations have become legendary. His message has changed thousands of lives around the globe. As the host of Motivational Minds Radio, Justin connects with the best of the best in spreading a message of hope and strength throughout the world.

Justin Sachs Coaching supports some of the most

successful corporate executives and entrepreneurs in the world as he works with them to create breakthrough results in their organizations and throughout their lives. His current projects include Ultimate Business Mastery, his signature event where he instructs entrepreneurs and small business leaders in taking their businesses to the next level through mastering their mindset for success and implementing specific action steps to enhance their marketing, sales, and media exposure.

Kate Daniels
aroundthetablegames.com

What began as a business of bringing families together through conversation has now brought the Daniels family together through entrepreneurship. Kate, daughter of Around the Table Games founder Beth Daniels, saw and heard the impact that her mom's games had on peoples' lives, so she decided to write some games of her own. Thanks to Kate's hard work, in 2009, Around the Table added Buddy Talk and Camp Talk to its line of award-winning conversation games. Kate was recently awarded the Young Toy and Game Inventor of the Year at the Chicago Toy and Game Fair 2010 for her creation of Buddy Talk and Camp Talk.

Keith J Davis Jr.
keithjdavisjr.com

Keith Davis, Jr. is a budding real estate agent, motivational speaker, author, undergraduate at the University of Houston, and the founder of K. Jerrold Enterprises, Inc., a personal empowerment company that serves as a catalyst for building economic-development programs for young leaders. Through thought-provoking seminars, writings, networking functions, and mentoring, K. Jerrold Enterprises, Inc. has inspired, educated, and motivated more than 3,000 young people to begin their transformational process to today's visionary leaders.

Khalil Parker
frenchwithfriends.weebly.com

Khalil DeBraux Parker is a twelve-year-old leader in the making. In January 2010, *The Washington Post* interviewed Khalil when he was the Student Government Association president for John Hanson French Immersion School. As a result of that article, Khalil received a personal invitation from the White House to meet President Barack Obama. "I will never forget when President Obama turned to my parents and said, 'You two have a very fine young man. He's definitely on the right path.'"

Khalil, who is also a published author, is now the president and CEO of French with Friends, LLC. Scheduled to launch in the summer of 2011, French with Friends, LLC is a full-service French tutoring company designed to help children enhance their French language skills. They offer introductory individual and small group sessions using a complete French curriculum that consists of vocabulary building, introductions, and understanding simple expressions. The one-hour sessions are comprised of individual or small group activities and games that are engaging, enlightening, and exciting.

Kohlfield Davis

Kohlfield Davis' early entrepreneurialism began at the age of twelve, when he purchased a broken Xbox 360, repaired it, then sold it for a profit. Kohlfield also has a passion for music and started playing in a restaurant with his band he started up. He has also built and sold his own guitars. He says if there's any one thing he'd like people to learn from his business success is that parents need to give kids credit. According to Kohlfield, kids have a lot more common sense than what most adults give them credit for. He says he's lucky his mom didn't underestimate his ability to start a business, and if more parents were like that, a lot more kids would start their businesses at a young age.

Kristyn Heath
passivedevices.com/us

Kristyn is a San Francisco Bay area native who graduated from Moreau Catholic High School. Now she is a junior at Santa Clara University's Leavey School of Business, where she is pursuing a major in business management. She has been very involved in the school's student-run multicultural center and had the opportunity to study abroad in Barcelona. She's also the inventor of NoeStringAttached, a music-sharing gadget that uses patent-pending technology that allows an unlimited number of people to share music from any type of portable music player (iPods, MP3 players, PSP, etc.). Her product has been featured on HGTV's *I Want That! Tech Toys*. She has been interviewed by MIT and NBC and received the most votes for MSNBC's Best Elevator Pitch of 2006, where she appeared as the youngest participant. She has won the *Black Enterprise* 2008 Teenpreneur Award and was featured in an issue of *Black Enterprise* magazine. Furthermore, she was the youngest CEO competitor and finalist in the 2008 Womens 2.0 conference, where she competed against 125 other women-owned companies. Kristyn gave business advice and encouragement to over 500 kids at the Black MBAs 2008 conference. Additionally, she was invited to speak at the 2009 Disney Dreamer's Academy, where she talked to one hundred high school students about her experience as a young entrepreneur. More recently, Kristyn has been promoting a new product—YBUDS, an earbud splitter. She has sold it at Santa Clara University's bookstore and online.

Lachlan Johnson
flipoutz.com

Lachlan Johnson and her siblings were the first youth entrepreneurs on ABC's *SharkTank* to showcase their Flipoutz business. She is currently a high school sophomore who relishes any new experience and likes to challenge herself. Her hobbies range from barrel racing to modeling and pageants, from filmmaking to sports. She has earned national recognition for historical documentaries and has earned varsity letters in volleyball and soccer. She was recently named first runner-up and most photogenic in the North Carolina Teen World pageant.

As a young entrepreneur, Lachlan enjoys her role as one of the Flipoutz spokespersons and creative directors. Although she still can't choose between the "Princess" coin or "Cowgirl Up", she feels very lucky to be able to enjoy it all.

**Lane Sutton
kidcriticusa.com**

Lane Sutton is a fourteen-year-old entrepreneur who has combined his knowledge of technology with his interest in business. He currently works as a social media strategist helping other companies use social media effectively for business. He speaks often on this topic to schools, companies, business professionals, colleges, and at conferences or events. Lane has been featured in *CNN, Forbes, The Boston Globe*, and many other media outlets and has been named a "boy wonder." Lane's first experiences in business started at age five, when he wrote and sold his own newspaper.

Bringing together his journalistic, technologic, and creative skills, Lane started KidCriticUSA.com, with reviews on products, restaurants, movies, and books that are kid and family friendly. He has built his brand, both online and off, not only through the power of social media including Facebook, LinkedIn, and Twitter, where he has more than 3,400 followers, but also through networking and making connections worldwide.

Lauren McClusky
nelarusky.com

Lauren McClusky began planning concerts at age sixteen when she founded McFest, a major charity initiative and concert series that benefits Special Olympics, in 2007. McFest, which is now called Nelarusky, has raised over $60,000 collectively through four annual concerts, with more on the way. Other than leading a team of young entrepreneurs in the planning stages of Nelarusky each year, Lauren has been both a part of the JMA (an independent promotion company in Chicago) intern program and has overseen key projects, including heading up JMA outreach at the Cornerstone Music Festival in Bushnell, Illinois. She has played a vital role in developing JMA's social networking strategy and remains extremely passionate about music and carrying out the JMA missions of excellence and service. A student at Boston University and now Columbia College Chicago studying music business, Lauren also spent a semester traveling on the Semester At Sea program.

Leanna Archer
leannashair.com

Leanna Archer, fifteen, is living her dream as CEO of Leanna's Inc., a hair and body products company that she started when she was nine years old. Initially, when her great grandmother made the product, Leanna would place samples in baby food bottles and sell them. Leanna's Inc. was created in 2005, and sells hair and body products online, as well as at some health food stores and beauty salons. She also has a Kid's Rep program, where kids can sell her products with their parent's help.

Lexi, Romi, Marni and Berni Barta
kidflicks.org

Lexi, Romi, Marni, and Berni Barta started Kid Flicks, a 501(c)(3) not-for-profit in 2002, when they were elementary, middle, and high school students. They had a lot of movies they no longer watched and decided to donate them to a local hospital where their friend had been treated for leukemia. When they dropped off their donations, they were told, "Movies are the first thing kids ask for when they are in the hospital." They decided to collect as many movies as possible and donate to as many hospitals as possible so that kids going through an experience that can be scary, lonely, boring, and/or painful would have a means of distraction. Over the last nine years, hardly a week has gone by that they have not received DVD donations from individuals, families, schools, churches, temples, movie studios, and other organizations from across the country. As of March 21, 2011, Kid Flicks has donated 57,600 movies to 576 hospitals in all fifty states and five hospitals in South Africa.

Lexxi Saal
lexxiloves.org

Lexxi Saal founded Lexxiloves.org when she was eight years old. Her foundation provides love and compassion to children in foster care. Lexxi raises funds to help children "Aging Out" of foster care and raises awareness about the effect this has on our society. Children who have aged out are sent into the world without the support of a loving family. Lexxi hopes to build several LexxiLoves.org houses to support the transition process for some of the 20,000 children who age out every year.

Lexxi is also a singer/songwriter and wrote an original song, "Thank You", as her tribute to the men and women in our military who make endless sacrifices to keep us safe. Lexxi's song has been included in several documentaries, and she performs for the many military men and women, both retired and currently active, at various ceremonies throughout the year. Lexxi has received several awards and medals from the United States Army for her tribute.

Lindsay Manseau
thatsocialthing.com

Lindsay Manseau is a freelance entrepreneur looking to make her big break. She's worked on a variety of projects since the age of fourteen, when she began as a photographer working for her mother's wedding photography business. At the age of twenty-one, she has worked on over five different entrepreneurial projects, including My Marriage Market, a web-based solution to help bridal couples and their vendors connect. Although that project wasn't the success she hoped it to be, she is planning to find success with social media marketing endeavors and to someday return to her first project. Her current focus is on helping small businesses in her local area while she studies small business and entrepreneurship at the University of Southern Maine.

Lizzie Marie Likness
lizziemariecuisine.com

Lizzie Likness started building her culinary empire at the age of six when she decided she wanted to pay for her own horse-riding lessons by selling all-natural snacks at a farmers market. She then expanded her business when her dad helped her create www.LizzieMarieCuisine.com, which allowed her to post her cooking videos to teach people worldwide how to have a delicious time cooking healthy meals. After winning a Del Monte Do Something Good for You! grant to teach cooking classes in her community, Lizzie was invited as a reporter and as a chef to Taste of Atlanta for three years in a row.

As a representative of the American Heart Association, Lizzie frequently speaks at different venues, teaching adults and children how to make healthier choices. The NFL Atlanta Falcons asked Lizzie to join them in their First Down for Fitness campaign, teaching students the importance of eating healthy and exercising on a daily basis. Recently, Lizzie was a guest on the *Rachael Ray* show and is currently starring in a series of videos for the launch of WebMD's new FIT website entitled "Healthy Cooking With Chef Lizzie." Lizzie's passion of helping families fight obesity continues to grow each year. As Lizzie says, "If a six year old can do something, so can you!"

Lorenzo Errico
formationskateboards.com

In the spring of 2004, Lorenzo Errico had a vision to start his own skateboard company. He brought that idea to life by creating the Formation Skateboard Company. His concept was, and still is, simple: to create unique high-quality skateboards. He began searching for visuals for his new project while attending Welsh Valley Middle School in Lower Merion, PA. He approached art teacher Todd Marrone. Marrone was already an established member of the local art community when Lorenzo invited him on board. Currently, Marrone continues to act as the art director of the Formation Skateboard Company, while Lorenzo continues to be the sole owner and operator and the sales and marketing director. In September 2008, Lorenzo enrolled in Drexel University's LeBow College of Business in Philadelphia, PA, working on completing a degree in entrepreneurship and marketing.

Mandee Widrick
mandeewidrick.com

Mandee Widrick is founder and CEO of ChargedUp Media, a social media marketing company. The idea for her social media business came as a direct result of her marketing endeavors for *Horse Family*™, an online magazine for equestrians that she created in January 2010. When business owners began to approach her asking for help with their social media profiles, presenting her with an opportunity to make money in both the horse and marketing industries, she jumped on it. As Mandee has found, sometimes when opportunity knocks all you need to do is open the door. Photo Credit: Tamika Diaz, Queen Diaz Photography of Watertown NY

Mary Sarah Gross
marysarahmusic.com

Not many just-turned 15-year olds are invited on stage by a legendary group like the Oak Ridge Boys to sing acapella. The captivated audience in Galveston's prestigious Opry sat enraptured... then came thunderous applause and a standing ovation for Mary Sarah's rendition of the 1961 Connie Frances hit, "Where the Boys Are," a song that most artists of her tender age would not even attempt, much less, know.

At 12, Mary Sarah toured the U.S. for 6 months as a featured lead vocalist and dancer in Kidz Bop, a Razor & Tie Records and Vee Corporation production, produced by Michael Anderson in Los Angeles. This was an 18-song rock concert from Kidz Bop albums, which to date have racked up 7 Gold albums, with "kid-friendly" cover versions of hits. The experience from performing in front of 4-6,000 kids per show defined her stage presence and earned her national and global popularity. After the Kidz Bop tour, Mary Sarah returned to Texas and began performing in local and regional Opry Theatres, Town Squares and Charity fundraisers.

Like many top country artists, Mary Sarah's first performances were in church at age 8. One advantage of living in Texas is the presence of hundreds of country radio stations and numerous regional Opry Theaters and Mary Sarah has performed in almost all of them multiple times, paying tribute to her heroes – the legends of country music.

174

Mary Sarah's album Crazy Good can be found on iTunes, recorded at the age of 14. She has recently sung the National Anthem for the Houston Astros Opening Day and will be a featured vocalist at the 2011 College World Series. This summer holds an entirely new project in Nashville with a release in fall of this year.

Mary Sarah is grounded in her faith and family traditions and asked at a very young age what she wanted for her future, "I want to be a voice for those who need one." I think she is well on her way.

**Matt Hackney
themov.org**

Matt Hackney started in business when he was a teen. He is now the founder of TheMOV, a progressive social network where Hackney teaches others many areas of the mind, body, and soul. As a fitness guru, martial artist, professional ballroom dancer, published author, computer programmer, and financial investor with a 44% annual ROI, Matt is a master of many trades and finds joy each day in sharing his secrets to success.

Matthew Turcotte
northshoresolutions.com

Matthew Turcotte founded North Shore Solutions when he was sixteen years old. What started as a hobby designing websites turned into a full-fledged business with an expansive team from across the globe that caters to clients from across the country. Turcotte published his own book, *From Main Street to Mainstream: The Essential Steps to Launching Your Small Town Business,* when he was a senior in high school. Turcotte is currently the first student to pioneer the Young Entrepreneurship Award program at Clarkson University, in which he is partnering with the university to grow his business further.

Melinda Marchiano
marchiano.net

Melinda Marchiano established her business, Happy Quail, in 2009. Her reasons for starting her business were not usual. Melinda became CEO of Happy Quail so that she would be able to publish the book she had written while she was recovering from cancer— without the harsh editing of a big publishing house. Believing her story needed to remain intact in order to truly help others with cancer, Melinda's Happy Quail published the first edition of *Grace* in October 2009. This first edition won two 2010 International Book Awards.

In January 2010, Melinda began working with Greenleaf Book Group on her second edition, *Grace: A Child's Intimate Journey Through Cancer and Recovery,* which Happy Quail published in October 2010. Her second edition is a finalist in the ForeWord Book of the Year Awards. Melinda is a passionate childhood cancer advocate, speaking at schools, cancer centers, cancer fundraisers, and many other events. Her associations include 2011 Livestrong Leader, Imerman Angel, childhood cancer writer for Fight Like a Girl Club, and dancer with the Civic Ballet of San Luis Obispo and San Luis Jazz.

Michael Costigan
speakingofmichael.com

Michael Costigan has traveled the world speaking to teens, is one of the nation's youngest CEOs, and he was recently named Entrepreneur of the Year by the National Financial Educators Council. As a thirteen year old, he set off to start his first business—madfusion. Written off and rejected by many for being too young or too inexperienced, he rose above skepticism to become what many said he never could. Now, years later, he strives to help teens face the very same issues he faced. Still young, he doesn't just relate to teens, he shares their experiences—their insecurities, their struggles, and the reality of growing up today.

An active member of the Association for Conflict Resolution and iSafe America, Michael brings knowledge and firsthand advice to every audience. Defined as a "young changemaker" by Youth Venture, a nonprofit that supports teen ventures, Michael delivers a message that is down to earth, inspiring, and exhilarating. Michael is also a regular columnist for RadicalParenting.com and YoungEntreprenuer.com.

Michael Kilby
subtletees.net

Michael Kilby is a high school student on the school cross-country and track teams, and he enjoys computer programming and graphic art, as well as word games and word play. His company, SubtleTeess began with an idea he developed after playing a word game with his family and completing an eighth-grade art project. He hopes to "get people thinking" with his designs, and enjoys hearing new ideas for his shirts. He designs, prints, and markets the T-shirts, and plans on saving his earnings for college, where he hopes to study computers/graphic design. He has been able to donate over $1,000 to charities and nonprofit organizations in the first year of running his business.

Michael Savage
redmetalbox.com

Michael Savage started Red Metal Box when he was sixteen years old. He currently focuses on building mobile applications for products such as the Apple's iPhone and iPod Touch. Michael has received several recognitions, such as the National Honor Roll of American Entrepreneurs. He is currently majoring in business administration at Campbell University and anticipates graduating in 2012.

Michael W. Montgomery
mikemonty.net

Michael Montgomery began his career as a yo-yo protégée at age thirteen. He competed in his first national yo-yo contest at age fourteen, founded and organized his own yo-yo contest at age fifteen, and launched his first business at age seventeen. No point in waiting when you know what you want to do when you grow up, right?

Today, he is still in love with all things yo-yos and has turned that passion into successful entrepreneurship. The Idaho State Yo-Yo Championships, which he founded, garnered media coverage from three Idaho television stations and multiple newspapers and has become an annual summer event in the great state of Idaho. Double-Take Industries, his "yo-yo centric" apparel company, is in full swing, and he also puts some of his considerable energy into helping others learn to use social media effectively. Michael does many yo-yo demonstrations every year for local schools, youth, and church organizations. He teaches the sport of yo-yoing online through his website YoYoTutorials.com and at various after-school programs. Michael still competes in the occasional yo-yo contest.

When he's not working on developing the sport and hobby of yo-yoing in Idaho, managing or creating new products for Double-Take Industries, or working on social media, Michael enjoys hanging out with his friends, watching the occasional movie, drawing, writing, and reading.

Nashely Ruiz
peppapeople.com

Nashely Ruiz was just seventeen when she started her own nonprofit PEPPA, People Educating People on Poverty Awareness. Inspired by her great-grandma Peppa, Nashely decided to take her hobby of craft making and sell handmade gifts. The Peppa organization donates all profit to help kids continue their education by buying school supplies, jackets, and shoes for economically challenged kids.

Nathaniel Marti
reflectyourlife.com

Nate Marti, fifteen, is the designer and business owner behind Reflections Apparel. A few years ago, Nate attended a summer entrepreneurship course through the Jacobsin Institute at the University of Iowa. That course allowed him to learn about business and develop start-up plans. He competed against other students in a business plan competition and won receiving cash as the prize. With those start-up funds, Nate launched his first legitimate business, which involved doing contracted artwork in the area of home portraits (popular with homeowners and real estate agents). Reflections Apparel sells T-shirts that, when reflected in the mirror, share inspirational thoughts and messages. A portion of every sale is given directly to various local and international charities.

Nick Ferguson
sustainfitness.com.au

Nick Ferguson started training athletes when he was very young. Now an elite cyclist and director of Sustain Fitness in Adelaide, Australia, Nick made the transition from athlete to instructor in 2006, after winning his first Australian cycling title, and has not looked back. Nick is passionate about helping people enjoy their lives through fitness. He has five years experience as a radio presenter and plays guitar in his spare time. Sustain Fitness works with individuals and organizations to help find a solution to improve health, fitness, and happiness through tailored training programs, skill development, and challenging activities. Sustain Fitness is currently developing into a new area: training the trainers. Through courses, resources, and consulting, Sustain Fitness–Education aims to help fitness professionals achieve greater success in the fitness industry.

Whether Nick is training, speaking, or educating, he provides a complete solution to the needs of his clients, inspiring and motivating them to commit to a change in their life for the better.

Nick Tart
juniorbiz.com
14clicks.com

Nick Tart, twenty-two, is a full-time entrepreneur from Colorado, who is passionate about helping young people with entrepreneurship. He's been "in like" with entrepreneurship since he started selling lemonade, golf balls, and bead animals at six years old. But he didn't fall in love with entrepreneurship until he saw a business plan competition during his sophomore year at Colorado State University. Since then he has dedicated his life to feeding entrepreneurial inspiration and advice to hungry young people who crave to be successful entrepreneurs.

Olivia Bennett
oliviabennett.com

Olivia Bennett is nationally recognized art prodigy who found her artistic gift at age 5, while battling A.L.L. Leukemia. What started as a hobby and emotional escape from her cancer treatment turned into a passion and full-time career. Olivia sold her first painting at the age of 8 and was excited to discover that someone loved her work enough to purchase it. From there, Olivia started showing her work at local art shows around Texas. At age 12, Olivia received national attention after her meeting with President Bush and her appearance on the Oprah Winfrey Show. In 2003, Olivia was named, "One of 20 Teens Who Will Change the World" by Teen People Magazine for her entrepreneurial and philanthropic work.

Olivia continued to travel and sell her work at shows and in gallery exhibits. At the age of 14, she opened the Olivia Bennett Art Gallery in Southlake, TX. She has one self-published book, "A Life in Full Bloom" and several other books featuring her artwork/story.

Now 21, Olivia currently lives in Southlake,Texas. Olivia currently teaches 30+ students weekly (middle/high school) and is very involved in the community. She currently supports many local and national charities including: Children's Cancer Fund, The Lance Armstrong Foundation and the Leukemia and Lymohoma Society. For more information about Olivia email sales@oliviabennett.com
Photo Credit: Wade Livingston

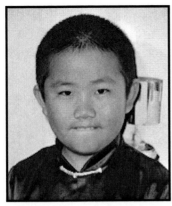

Perry Chen
perryspreviews.com

Perry Chen was only eight when his first movie review using a kid-friendly starfish rating system was published in a San Diego newspaper. A few months later, his national TV debut on *CBS Evening News with Katie Couric* as America's youngest film critic made him an overnight sensation. Since then, this pint-sized creative force of nature has been unstoppable, interviewing Oscar-winning directors on the red carpet, winning prestigious press club awards, speaking at a TEDx Conference, hosting a radio talk show, reviewing restaurants, acting in commercials, and now, becoming a filmmaker and animator himself, collaborating with twice Oscar-nominated animator Bill Plympton in an animation short about a young Holocaust survivor. *Ingrid Pitt: Beyond the Forest* will premiere at various film festivals around the world in 2011.

When asked about his advice for children and youth, Perry said, "If you believe, you can achieve! You're never too young to start pursuing your dreams and passion!" No doubt, this fifth grader has five "Perrific!" starfish all over his path.

Quinn van der Gulik
quinnvandergulik.com

As a three-year-old boy, Quinn, started his first lemonade-stand business. His first venture was a huge success and he not only learned about salesmanship and customer service, but he also learned his first lesson in giving back to society by donating part of his profits to children less fortunate than himself. His second business was a dismal failure, but instead of giving up, Quinn used his creative ingenuity to turn his new venture back into a great success.

Rachel Pavelka
everygirlzdream.webs.com
pavpackacres.webs.com

Rachel Pavelka, age sixteen, has owned multiple businesses since the age of six. She and her three siblings have owned thirty businesses over the last ten years, with Rachel being the driving force behind most of them. Rachel is an energetic entrepreneur who enjoys customer service and providing quality products for her customers. Her goal in life is to train other teens and tweens on how to own their own businesses. Currently she owns Every Girlz Dream Jewelry Company, which imports beautiful jewelry from Peru, which in turn helps the local artisans live a better life, and Pavpack Acres, which is a small kennel that raises well-adjusted and well-loved Malteses and Morkies.

Reed Floren
reedfloren.com

Reed Floren has been marketing online since back in 1999, when he was thirteen. Over the years he's had many trials and triumphs, and now travels all over the world sharing his story and inspiring entrepreneurs across the United States, Canada, United Kingdom, New Zealand, Australia, Malaysia, Singapore, and Hong Kong.

Robert Van Hoessel
robertvanhoesel.com

Robert van Hoesel started off as many young entrepreneurs do. At age fourteen he began designing and building webpages for clients in the music scene. In a short amount of time, Robert transformed himself into a public speaker and started his own foundation for Dutch young entrepreneurs, becoming one of the role models for many talented teenagers in Holland. And his business? Robert, now seventeen, has a consultancy company, where he and the freelancers he hires advise companies involved in youth communication.
Photo Credit: Ridderhof

Ryan Bertrand
appbeastinc.com

Ryan Bertrand started designing websites when he was fifteen years old. He started by developing a website for a local taqueria, then went on to design a few more websites, and eventually landed an intern position at a nice firm, Blast Advanced Media. Ryan released his first app when he was seventeen. It was a creative prank-call app that allowed you to fake a call to get out of a bad date or whatnot. While he was interning at Blast Advanced Media, the boss asked him to make a Google Analytics iPhone app. It started as a free app with about five Google Analytics reports and grew into an app with sixty-five reports and features their competition cannot keep up with. Eventually this led him to getting hired by Blast Advanced Media as a web developer/API specialist. A few months ago, BAM Analytics won the "Google Developer Idol" competition.

Ryan Coisson
ryancoisson.com

From the time he was a young kid, Ryan Coisson would buy and resell bulk candy to the kids at school. Now, seventeen years and many businesses later, he is still working for himself. Ryan is an Internet-based entrepreneur who specializes in search engine optimization and search engine marketing. He also helps clients with information marketing and lead generation.
Photo Credit: Morgan Trinker

Ryan Ross
tinytrump.com

Ryan Ross started his first business when he was three years old. He sold eggs at church in Vernon, BC, Canada. His baby brother was very ill and his family decided to only eat food they grew themselves. Ryan decided that if he raised chickens, he could give his brother fresh eggs, but he could also sell the eggs for a good profit and help pay for some of his special needs.

Rydel Hemmings
rydelsadventure.com

Rydel Hemmings is fifteen years old and living the dream. She has already traveled for over thirty months total. Rydel is a travel writer and blogger and makes money selling an e-book she has written on how kids can make money.

Sabirul Islam
sabirulislam.com
theworldatyourfeet.com

Sabirul Islam, a teen-trepreneur from the age of just fourteen, is a global motivational speaker, having spoken at over 600 events, and author of the best-selling book, *The World at Your Feet at 17*. Sabirul's vision is to inspire millions of young people around the world that ordinary people can become extraordinary.

With Sabirul becoming a trader at sixteen and his inspiring book selling over 42,500 copies across the UK, Sabirul launched his Teen-Trepreneur business board game that educates young people about becoming future tycoons. Now aged twenty, Sabirul's vision to inspire young people has expanded on a global scale, having arranged tours reaching out to people in USA, Nigeria, South Africa, and across Europe. This inspired Sabirul to launch Teen-Speakers, bringing together the world's most successful youth onto a single speaking platform. Sabirul is a teen-trepreneur who aims to bring success to the heart of today's youth.

Savannah Britt
girlpez.com

Savannah Britt is the 17 year-old socialite turned entrepreneur who is taking the entertainment industry by storm. At the age of eight, Britt wrote and published her first writing piece, a poem on www.poetry.com as well as its bounded issue. Throughout 2004-2005 she was hired as a paid published writer as a book reviewer for "The Kitchen Table News" which had a readership of 70,000. She then developed a website for girls ages 12-16, www.girlpez.com. Accompanying the site Girlpez is a hard copy magazine entitled Girlpez Fashion Magazine. The magazine has recently transitioned from print to being online only. The magazine has been seen and endorsed by some of the top people in the industry such as Amy Astley, the editor in chief of Teen Vogue. Britt is a serious socialite, as she is becoming a red carpet favorite. She's been seen reporting and providing coverage at different concert venues for some of today's top stars such as Chris Brown, Sean Kingston, Lil Wayne, and Leona Lewis! Along with that she has interviewed stars such as Shwayze, Kevin Rudolf, and Shawty Putt.

Sean Coleman
orangeslyce.com

Sean Coleman graduated magna cum laude from Arizona State University in 2009 with a B.S.E in Computer Systems Engineering. With an extensive background in technology entrepreneurship, Sean successfully ran a profitable web design firm for over five years, which he began as a teen, developing extensive business relationships with hundreds of clients. As an undegraduate student, Sean completed his Honors thesis, "When Open Source Works: Criteria for Gauging Open Source Adoption Success", under the mentorship of ASU's University Technology Officer Adrian Sannier. In conjuntion with his thesis, Sean was awarded a research contract from the Arizona Department of Transportation to investigate utilizing Open Source Software. Sean has been selected for numerous entrepreneurship awards, including the Arizona Republic's "35 Entrepreneurs 35 and Younger" in 2009, and the Small Business Administration's "Young Entrepreneur of the Year" for Arizona.

Shama Hyder
marketingzen.com

Shama Hyder began her journey in entrepreneurship when she was in elementary school selling wrapping paper and gift cards. Now she is a web and TV personality, best-selling author, international speaker, and award-winning CEO of The Marketing Zen Group, a global digital marketing firm. Shama is the face of today's digital world and represents the best her generation has to offer. She has aptly been dubbed the "master millennial of the universe" and "an online marketing shaman" by FastCompany.com.

Shama holds a masters degree in organizational communication from the University of Texas at Austin, and prides herself in being a constant learner. Through her web marketing company, Shama works with businesses and organizations around the world. In 2009, *Business Week* honored Shama as one of the Top 25 under 25 entrepreneurs in North America. In 2010, Shama won the prestigious Technology Titan Emerging Company CEO award. Her first book, *The Zen of Social Media Marketing* (BenBella Books), was released in April 2010, and was an instant hit. When not working directly with her clients or shooting her show, Shama travels the world speaking on business, entrepreneurship, and technology.

Shane Hudson
shanehudson.net

Teen entrepreneur Shane Hudson is the founding author of Success Circuit, a website that inspires and motivates readers to actually *do* something. Inspiration can come in many forms, and Shane interviews inspirational people. Not all of them are rich and/or famous. Shane believes that every person on this planet is inspiring in their own way. Aside from Success Circuit, he also does a lot of website development and programming.

Stanley Tang
stanleytang.com

Stanley Tang started his first Internet business when he was just thirteen years old. Since then, he has worked on several projects, including an online magazine and a social news reader. He also published a book on the topic of Internet entrepreneurship called *eMillions*, which was a bestseller on Amazon in four categories. He is now a student studying at Stanford.

Stephen Ou
stephenou.com
ohboard.com
labs.stephenou.com/
itunes
twtroulette.com
oneextralap.com

It only took a year for Stephen Ou to make his software business profitable. He is now sixteen years old and has created four popular online software applications, including OhBoard, iTunes Instant, TwtRoulette, and OneExtraLap. His apps were featured by well-known publications such as *Forbes, Business Insider, Fast Company, TechCrunch, Mashable,* and more. Stephen was named as one of the "5 Teen Entrepreneurs to Watch in 2011" and "10 Inspirational Entrepreneurs 21 and Under."

Steven Gordon
thetattooid.com

When he was a teenager, Steven Gordon created TattooID (pronounced tat-too-eed), which provides parents with safe, fun, temporary tattoo identities for their children, featuring their initials and contact information. In the summer of 2009, Steven participated in NFTE's two-week summer BizCamp at Columbia University, which inspired him to create a business plan based on his experience with his little brother getting lost. When he learned that 1.3 million children are reported missing each year, he created a solution. He envisions a day in which he can not only save children, but save the world.

Steven Haggerty

From a young age, Steven Haggerty had shown interest in business, from selling CDs to his friends at school to starting an online radio. He started to do website design as a hobby when he was about fourteen, and that blossomed into Salut World, a web design and hosting company. He has since sold Salut World and is traveling the world.

Suzanna Duly
zazzle.com/upnorthfun

Suzanna Duly was fourteen years old when her father asked her to create a fun T-shirt design for the family to wear at their vacation lake spot in Michigan. The family came up with a fun "Top 10 Things Heard on the Lake". It was just a fun family project. But each time her family wore the T-shirts out in public, they were stopped and asked about them. That family project soon became Suzanna's business, North Shore T-Shirts, with many more ideas and many more areas of Michigan covered. Suzanna has been having fun ever since making money toward her first car and college.

Sydney Powell
ssbrandz.yolasite.com

Sydney Powell's journey into youth entrepreneurship happened more at the prodding of her mother, Melissa, than by pure self-motivation. A fourth-generation entrepreneur, Sydney had natural business instincts and leadership skills, but she lacked the knowledge to take full advantage of them. At age twelve, she and her two friends, Shelby and Veronica, opened their first business called Plants, Paws & Pacifiers. A year later, The Browny Company, a gourmet, made-to-order brownie company, and Ragz Clothing Exchange, a teen clothing exchange, were formed. Sydney continues to run her businesses and is always on the lookout for more opportunities. They now run all of their companies under the name, SS Brandz.

Sydney, now fifteen, is also an avid volunteer and has been helping kids in her community since the fourth grade. She's been the community service officer for her business club, a co-founder of an anti-bullying club at her school, and a member of Key Club. She is also a volunteer with The Friendship Circle, where she's a mentor for physically and mentally challenged youth. In her spare time, she loves to read, play sports, listen to all types of music, and just hang out with friends.

Tiffanie, Twana, and Victoria Williams
drivesafesigns.com

Professional dancers, actors, models, singers, inventors, social entrepreneurs, and new recording artists G-Wiz, the Williams sisters—Tiffanie, Twana, and Victoria—are reducing road and highway fatalities as co-founders of their award-winning organization "Smart Teens Drive Safe". Recipients of numerous local and national awards like the prestigious Palmetto Center for Women (formally the YWCA) TWIN Award, *Black Enterprise* Teen Preneurs of the Year, Merrill Lynch Young Entrepreneurs Award, and recently awarded the Order of the Palmetto (highest civilian award given for service in the state of South Carolina), they were also presented the Key to the City of Columbia, with a proclamation naming May as "Smart Teens Drive Safe Month". These young entrepreneurs have also been featured in numerous local and national magazines (reaching as far as Shanghai China), such as *Black Enterprise, Imara Woman* magazine, *Seventeen,* and *Guideposts Sweet 16* magazine. They've also made the front business section of the state newspaper; have been featured in a book written by Jon Swartz, money market reporter for *USA Today,* and in a documentary.

The Williams sisters recently made history again being the first teenage singing group assigned to the Universal/CMG Record Label. In addition, these young ladies have won local and national titles in the entertainment industry as former artist Triple Threat, and now new recording artist G-Wiz.

Travis Woodward
dinosoarstudios.com

At age fourteen, Travis Woodward and his friends used to play around with a video camera making movies. He quickly learned how to take the video and create stories with movement, music, and exciting features. The following summer he told his mom that instead of working at the mall for his summer job, he wanted to start his own business. Born and raised in San Jose, California, and a student of Bellarmine College Preparatory, Travis owns a successful video production company called, "Dinosoar Studios, We make your ideas SOAR!"

Xanthe van der Gulik
xanthevandergulik.com

At the young age of just five years old, Xanthe began her journey in learning about the value of money from earning a penny for each bag she folded for her grandmother. She eventually learned that she could earn more while having more fun following her own true passions. Xanthe's story is not only a great way to teach children about the value of money, but it is also an incredible inspiration to other kids that they too can earn their own money by doing the things they love!

Zachery Collins
zacktheweb.com

Zachary Collins was fourteen years old when he first started realizing the power of the Internet. He started out on GeoCities, once a website creator owned by Yahoo. As he spent more and more time discovering the entrepreneurial tricks of the Internet, he started his first major website called Twtbase, which was a Twitter applications database and home to the very first Twitter application search engine, which was later sold for a few thousand dollars. Over time, he created some other popular websites that he then sold, such as Yazzem (which he is best known for) and his overnight hits, Mabzy, a website for checking in to websites, and RebuzzThis, which served millions of Google Buzz share buttons a day. Now he's sixteen and working on some really big ideas.

Zack Gonzalez
zackgonzalez.com

Zack Gonzalez is an internationally-known American activist for autism, a stand-up comedian, and the best-selling author of the award-winning memoir, *Saving Deets!,* and the newly released *Charity Bites!* and *Teen-Social Entrepreneur,* among many other books. He currently hosts his own show, *It's on with Zack,* which began in July 2009. Zack was also named one of 2009's Inspirational Teens. He's been on autism shows, such as Autism-Talk Radio and Hope Saves the Day. The comedian also recently began his own production company called Zack G. Comedy Productions.

Zack supports and has raised funds for a large variety of autism charities. In addition, he currently owns and manages his own clothing line, AUTISM AWARENESS by Zack, and is the creator of the Play Now for Autism and Laugh Now for Autism event-chains benefiting autism research and aid for families affected by autism.

He has one brother with autism (diagnosed in 2005) and claims that Ethan AKA Deets is his "main inspiration" for everything he does. Zack was born, raised, and currently resides in Los Angeles, CA.

Zack Gooding
guiltlessgiving.com

Zack Gooding started Guiltless Giving in 2007, when he was nine years old. He also created the Dare to Care Kit for a school invention project, which is a hygiene kit with basics necessities, such as toothbrush, toothpaste, soap, deodorant, comb, and an information card (with phone numbers to get help), to hand out to people who are homeless. "Giving out kits is a great way for people to help someone who is homeless without giving money or ignoring him/her," says Zack. "We keep Dare to Care kits in our glove box and give them out when we see a homeless person. It feels good to help people who are down and out with items they can use."

Zack Hix
goodboyroy.com

Good Boy Roy is a fun line of character T-shirts all created and drawn by sixteen-year-old Zack Hix. Zack was fourteen when he created the first character, Roy. His mom had that original design printed onto a shirt for him. He loved it, and so did a lot of other people. This turned into a "lightbulb" moment for them both, and more characters were created and the new line was born. Zack has always loved to draw and create cartoons, but drawing was more than fun for him, it was therapeutic as well. You see, Zack struggles with challenging emotional/neurological difficulties and his drawing allowed him to diffuse some of the inner emotional turmoil at times. Zack hopes to be an inspiration to kids everywhere and show that nothing is impossible. The creation of Good Boy Roy has brought smiles to many. The characters are fun, kid friendly, and a personality most of us know. Zack dreams that someday the Good Boy Roy line will be a recognizable brand on everything from mugs to tire covers, and a cartoon show, with Zack being the voice of Roy.

Resource List
Curriculum

Biz at Bedtime
http://www.bizatbedtime.com/

Biz Gym
http://www.bizgym.com/

Biz in a Boxx
http://www.bizinaboxx.com/

Bouje Publishing
http://www.boujepublishing.com/

BSchool
http://www.bschool.com/little-entrepreneurs-business-for-kids/

Business News For Kids
http://www.businessnewsforkids.com/

Independent Youth
http://www.independentyouth.org/

Junior Achievement
http://mybusiness.ja.org/
http://newstudentcenter.ja.org

TREPS
http://www.trepsed.com/

Young Biz
http://www.youngbiz.com/

Business Organizations

Ashoka's Youth Venture
http://genv.net/

The BizWorld Foundation
http://bizworld.org/

Collegiate Entrepreneurs' Organization
http://c-e-o.org/

Consortium for Entrepreneurship Education
http://entre-ed.org/

Corporation for Enterprise Development
http://cfed.org/programs/youth_entrepreneurship

DECA
http://deca.org/

Future Business Leaders of America
http://fbla.org/

Global Student Entrepreneur Awards
http://gsea.org/

Junior Achievement
http://ja.org/

Network For Teaching Entrepreneurship
http://nfte.com/

Secret Millionaires Club
http://smckids.com/

Young Entrepreneur Council
http://youngentrepreneurcouncil.com/

Entrepreneurship Websites

14 Clicks
http://14clicks.com

Biz Launch
http://bizlaunch.com/

Blogtrepreneur
http://blogtrepreneur.com

Business Opportunities Weblog Network
http://business-opportunities.biz/

Business Week
http://businessweek.com/

Centre for Entrepreneurship Education and Development
http://ceed.info/

CEO Express
http://ceoexpress.com/default.asp

Entrepreneur magazine
http://entrepreneur.com

Epic Launch
http://epiclaunch.com/

Extreme Entrepreneurship Tour
http://extremetour.org/

Future Business Leaders of America
http://fbla-pbl.org

Future CEO Stars
http://fcsmag.com/

Homeschool Entrepreneur
http://homeschoolent.com/

Inc. magazine
http://inc.com

Independent Means Inc.
http://independentmeans.com/imi/index.php

Micro Business for Teens
http://microbusinessforteens.com

Millionaire Secrets
http://millionairesecrets.com/

Mind Your Own Business
http://mindyourownbiz.org/default.shtml

Mixergy
http://mixergy.com/

MySmallBiz.com
http://mysmallbiz.com/teen-business

Quick Sprout
http://quicksprout.com/

Quintessential Careers
http://quintcareers.com/younger_teen_job_dos-donts.html

Renegade CEOs
http://renegadeceos.com/

Retire @ 21
http://retireat21.com/

The Student Success Manifesto
http://successmanifesto.com/

Success magazine
http://successmagazine.com/

Teen Business Forum
http://teenbusinessforum.com/

Under 30 CEO
http://under30ceo.com/

Unstrapp'd
http://unstrappd.com/

Young Biz
http://youngbiz.com/

Young Entrepreneur
http://youngentrepreneur.com

Young Pre Pro
http://youngprepro.com/

Youth Action Net
http://youthactionnet.org/

Ypulse
http://ypulse.com

Funding and Finance

Business Finance
http://businessfinance.com/

FamZoo
http://FamZoo.com

Funding Universe
http://fundinguniverse.com/

IndieGoGo
http://indiegogo.com/

KickStarter
http://kickstarter.com/

Kidnexions
http://kidnexions.com/

LearnVest
http://learnvest.com/

Money Trail
http://www.moneytrail.net/

National Financial Educators Council
http://financialeducatorscouncil.org/

Peer Backers
http://peerbackers.com

Rocket Hub
http://rockethub.com/

U.S. Small Business Administration
http://sba.gov/

Young Money
http://youngmoney.com/

The Zela Wela Kids
http://zelawelakids.com

Tax and Legal

Corp Net
http://www.corpnet.com/

Ernest Grumbles
http://www.ernestgrumbles.com/

Family Wealth Planning Institute
http://familywealthmatters.com

Legal Zoom
http://legalzoom.com/

Tiernan and Associates
http://tiernanassoc.com/

Tech & New Media

Grasshopper
http://grasshopper.com/

Mashable
http://mashable.com/

Social Media Examiner
http://socialmediaexaminer.com

TechCrunch
http://techcrunch.com/

Wired
http://wired.com/

Connecting With Others

http://Facebook.com
http://LinkedIn.com
http://Twitter.com
http://YouTube.com

Other Resources We Love

About One
http://aboutone.com

Inside Track: College Admissions
http://collegeadmissions.insidetrack.com

Mail Chimp
http://mailchimp.com

Small Business Marketing
http://www.marketingbestpractices.com/

Vista Print
http://vistaprint.com

More resources we love can be found at
http://RaisingCEOKids.com/ReliableResources

QR code on page 33:
http://raisingceokids.com/unique/

QR code on page 35:
http://raisingceokids.com/nominate/

QR code on page 62:
http://raisingceokids.com/attitude/

QR code on page 74:
http://raisingceokids.com/internship-program/